Margaret Oliphant

Kirsteen

The story of a Scotch family seventy years ago. Vol. 2

Margaret Oliphant

Kirsteen

The story of a Scotch family seventy years ago. Vol. 2

ISBN/EAN: 9783337411244

Printed in Europe, USA, Canada, Australia, Japan

Cover: Foto ©ninafisch / pixelio.de

More available books at **www.hansebooks.com**

BY
MRS. OLIPHANT

IN THREE VOLUMES
VOL. II

London
MACMILLAN AND CO.
AND NEW YORK
1890

The Right of Translation and Reproduction is Reserved

KIRSTEEN.

CHAPTER I.

THE 12th of January was a still, gray winter day, not very cold and exceedingly calm, the winds all hushed, the clouds hanging low, with a possibility of rain—a possibility which is never remote in a Highland landscape. As the slow daylight began to bring the hills into sight, not with any joyous sunrising but with a faint diffusion of gray upon the dark, a gradual growing visible of the greater points, then very slowly of the details of the landscape, there came also into sight, first ghost-like, a moving, noiseless shadow, then something which consolidated into the slim figure of a woman, a solitary traveller moving steadily along the dewy mountain road. It came in sight like the hills, not like an interruption to the landscape but a portion of it, becoming visible along with it, having been in the dark as well as in the light. Before the day was fully awake it was there, a gliding shadow going straight up the hills and over the moors, at the same measured pace, not so much quick as steady, with a wonderful still intensity of progress. The road was more than dewy, it was glistening wet with the heavy damps of the night, every crevice among the rocks green and sodden, every stone glistening. The traveller did not keep exactly to the road, was not afraid of the wet hillside turf, nor even of a gray dyke to climb if it shortened the way. She passed lightly over bits of moss among the rustling, faded heather, and spots of suspicious greenness which meant bog, choosing her footing on the black roots of the wild myrtle, and the knolls of blackberries, like one to the manner born. She gave a soul to the wild and green landscape, so lonely, so washed with morning dews. She was going—where? From the impossible to the possible—from the solitudes of the hills into the world.

Kirsteen had been walking for hours before she thus came into sight, and the dark and the silence had filled her with many a flutter of terror. It took something from what might have been in other circumstances the overwhelming excitement of thus leaving home to encounter that other bewildering and awful sensation of going out into the night, with every one asleep and all wrapped in the profound blackness of winter, through which it was hard enough even for the most familiar to find a way. This horror and alarm had so occupied her mind, and the sensation of being the one creature moving and conscious in that world of darkness that she had scarcely realized the severance she was making, the tearing asunder of her life. Even Marg'ret, repressing her emotion lest a sob should catch some wakeful ear in the sleeping house, had faded from Kirsteen's mind when she took the first step into the dark. She knew there were no wild beasts who could devour her, no robbers who would seize her, as she had fancied when a child: she had a trembling sense that God would protect her from ghosts and spiritual evils; but her young soul trembled with fears both physical and spiritual, just as much as when she had wandered out in the dark at six years old. Reason convinces but does not always support the inexperienced spirit. When the ever wakeful dogs at the little clachan heard the faint footfall upon the edge of the path and barked, Kirsteen was half-consoled and half-maddened with terror. If some one should wake and wonder, and suspect a midnight thief, and burst open a door and find her; but on the other hand it was a little comfort to feel that even a dog was waking in that black expanse of night.

She had already come a long way, before the daylight, when she and the landscape that inclosed her came dimly, faintly into sight in the first grey of the morning. Her eyes had got accustomed to the darkness, her heart a little calmed and sustained by the fact that nothing had happened to her yet, no hidden malefactor in the dark, nor sheeted whiteness from the churchyard interrupting her on her way. Her heart had beat while she passed, loud enough to have wakened the whole clachan, but nothing had stirred, save the dogs—and safe as in the warmest daylight she had got by the graves. Nothing could be so bad as that again. Partly by familiar knowledge and partly by the consciousness of certain gradations in the darkness as she became used to it, she had got forward on her way until she had reached the head of the loch where the water was a guide to her. Kirsteen had resolved that she would not venture to approach the town or cross the loch in the boat, the usual way, but taking a large sweep round the end of the loch, strike at once into the wilds which lay between her and the comparatively higher civilization of the regions within reach of Glasgow. If she could but reach that great city, which was only second in her dim conceptions to London itself, she would feel that she was safe, but not before. She came round the head of the loch in the beginnings of the dawn and had pushed her way far into the gloomy mystery of Hell's Glen, with its bare hills rising to the dim sky on either side, before the height of noon. It is gloomy there even when the height of noon means the dazzling of a Highland summer day. But when the best of the daylight is a dull gray, the long lines of the glen, unbroken by anything but a shepherd's hut here and there at long intervals, and the road that could be seen winding through like a strip of ribbon all the way gave the fugitive a mingled sense of serenity and of that tingling, audible solitude and remoteness from all living aid or society which thrills every nerve. When she was half way through the glen, however, the thrill was subdued by that experience of no harm as yet which is the most perfect of support, and Kirsteen began to be conscious that she had eaten nothing and scarcely rested since she set out. She had swallowed a mouthful as she walked—she had thrown herself down for a moment on the hillside—but now it seemed possible to venture upon a little real rest.

Kirsteen was dressed in a dark woollen gown of homespun stuff, made like all the dresses of the time, with a straight, long, narrow skirt, and a short bodice cut low round her shoulders. Over this she had a warm spencer, another bodice with long sleeves, rising to her throat, where it was finished with a frill. She had strong country shoes and woollen stockings just visible under her skirt. Her bonnet was a little of the coal scuttle shape but not very large; and flung back over it, but so that she could put it down over her face at a moment's notice, was a large black veil, such an imitation of Spanish lace as was practicable at the time, better in workmanship, worse in material than anything we have now. The large pattern with its gigantic flowers in thick work hid the face better than any lighter fabric, and it hung over the bonnet when thrown back like a cloud. She had a bundle on one arm, done up carefully in a handkerchief containing two changes of linen, and another gown, carefully folded by Marg'ret into the smallest possible space; and on the other a camlet cloak, dark blue, with a fur collar and metal clasps, which was Marg'ret's own. This was sore lading for a long walk, but it was indispensable in face of the January winds, and the cold on the coach, of which Marg'ret knew dreadful things. To Kirsteen it seemed that if she could but reach that coach, and pursue her journey by the aid of other legs than her own, and with company, all her troubles would be over. She sat upon the hillside anxiously watching the path lest any suspicious figure should appear upon it, and took out from her wallet the last scones of Marg'ret's she was likely to eat for a long time. Should she ever eat Marg'ret's scones again? Salt tears came to Kirsteen's eyes and moistened her comely face. It was done now—the dreadful step taken, never to be altered, the parting made. Her life and her home lay far behind her, away beyond the hills that shut her in on every side. She said to herself with trembling lips that the worst was over; by this time every one in Drumcarro would know that she was gone. They would have looked for her in every corner, up on the hill and down by the linn where the water poured into the vexed and foaming gulf. Would it come into anybody's head that she had thrown herself in and made an end of everything?

"The only art her guilt to cover."

Would they send and tell Glendochart, poor old gentleman—would they warn him not to come to a distressed house? Or would he be allowed to come and her father say to him: "She is not worthy of a thought. She is no bairn of mine from this day"? "And my mother will go to her bed," said Kirsteen to herself with a tear or two, yet with the faint gleam of a smile. She could see them all in their different ways—her father raging, her mother weeping, and Mary telling everybody that she was not surprised. And Marg'ret—Marg'ret would put on a steady countenance so that nobody could tell what she knew and what she didn't know. It almost amused Kirsteen though it made her breath come quick, and brought the tears to her eyes, to sit thus in the deep solitude with the silence of the hills all thrilling round, and look down as it were upon that other scene, a strangely interested spectator, seeing everything, and her own absence which was the strangest of all.

But perhaps she sat too long and thought too much, or the damp of the sod had cramped her young limbs, or the tremendous walk of the morning told more after an interval of rest, for when she roused herself at last and got up again, Kirsteen felt a universal ache through her frame, and stumbled as she came down from her perch to the road below. How was she to get through Glencroe to Arrochar—another long and weary course? The solitude of the glen came upon her again with a thrill of horror.

If she could not walk any better than this it would be dark, dark night again before she came to the end of her journey—would she ever come to the end of her journey? Would she drop down upon the hill and lie there till some one found her? A wave of discouragement and misery came over her. There was a house within sight, one of those hovels in which still the Highland shepherd or crofter is content to live. Kirsteen knew such interiors well—the clay floor, the black, smoke-darkened walls, the throng of children round the fire: there was no room to take in a stranger, no way of getting help for her to push on with her journey. All the pictures of imagination fled from her, scant and troubled though they had been. Everything in the world seemed wept out except the sensation of this wild solitude, the aching of her tired limbs, the impossibility of getting on, her own dreadful loneliness and helplessness in this wild, silent, unresponsive world.

Kirsteen could scarcely tell how she dragged herself to the entrance of the glen.

A little solitary mountain farm or gillie's house stood at some distance from the road, approached by a muddy cart-track. The road was bad enough, not much more than a track, for there were as yet no tourists (nay, no magician to send them thither) in those days. A rough cart came lumbering down this path as she crept her way along, and soon made up to her. Kirsteen had made up her mind to ask for a " cast " or "lift " to help her along, but her courage failed her when the moment came, and she allowed the rude vehicle to lumber past with a heart that ached as much as her limbs to see this chance of ease slip by. She endeavoured as much as she could to keep within a certain distance of the cart " for company," to cheat the overwhelming loneliness which had come over her. And perhaps the carter, who was an elderly rustic with grizzled hair, perceived her meaning, perhaps he saw the longing look in her eyes. After he had gone on a little way he turned and came slowly back. " Maybe you're ower genteel for the like of that," he said, " but I would sooner ye thought me impident than leave you your lane on this rough long road. Would you like a lift in the cart? There's clean straw in it, and you're looking weariet."

Poor Kirsteen had nearly wept for pleasure. She seated herself upon the clean straw with a sense of comfort which no carriage could have surpassed. It was a mode of conveyance not unknown to her. The gig had seldom been vouchsafed to the use of the girls in Drumcarro. They had much more often been packed into the cart. She thanked the friendly carter with all her heart. " For I am weariet," she said, " and the road's wet and heavy both for man and beast."

" Ye'll have come a far way," he said, evidently feeling that desire for information or amusement which unexpected company is wont to raise in the rustic heart.

Kirsteen answered that she had come from a little place not far from Loch Fyne, then trembled lest she had betrayed herself.

" It's very Hieland up there," said the

carter; "that's the country of the Lord their God the Duke, as Robbie Burns calls him. We have him here too, but no so overpowering. Ye'll be a Campbell when you're at hame."

"No, I am not a Campbell," said Kirsteen. It occurred to her for the first time that she must give some account of herself. "I'm going," she said, "to take up—a situation."

"I just thought that. 'Twill be some pingling trade like showing or hearing weans their letters, keeping ye in the house and on a seat the haill day long."

"Something of that kind," Kirsteen said.

"And you're a country lass, and used to the air of the hills. Take you care—oh, take care! I had one mysel'—as fine a lass as ye would see, with roses on her cheeks, and eyes just glancing bright like your ain; and as weel and as hearty as could be. But before a twelvemonth was o'er, her mother and me we had to bring her hame."

"Oh," cried Kirsteen, "I am very sorry—but she's maybe better."

"Ay, she's better," said the carter. "Weel —wi' her Faither which is in heaven."

"Oh, I'm sorry, sorry!" cried Kirsteen, with tears in her eyes.

"Thank ye for that: ye have a look of her: I couldna pass ye by: but eh, for Gudesake if ye have faither and mother to break their hearts for you, take care."

"You must have liked her well, well!" said the girl. Fatigue and languor in herself added to the keen sense of sympathy and pity. "I wish it had been me instead of her," she said hastily.

"Eh," said the man, "that's a sair thing to say! Ye must be an orphan with none to set their hearts on you—but you're young, poor thing, and there's nae telling what good may come to ye. Ye must not let down your heart."

The cart rumbled on with many a jolt, the carter jogged by the side and talked, the sound and motion were both drowsy, and Kirsteen was extremely tired. By and by these sounds and sensations melted into a haze of almost beatitude, the drowsiness that comes over tired limbs and spirit when comparative ease succeeds to toil. After a while she lost consciousness altogether and slept nestled in the straw, like a tired child. She was awakened by the stoppage of the cart, and opening her eyes to the gray yet soft heavens above and the wonder of waking in the open air, found herself at the end of a road which led up to a farmstead at the mouth of Glencroe where the valley opens out upon the shore of that long inlet of the sea which is called Loch Long.

"I'm wae to disturb ye, but I must take the cairt back to the town, and my ain house is two miles down the loch. But there's a real dacent woman at the inn at Arrochar."

"It's there I was going," said Kirsteen hurriedly sliding from her place. She had been covered with her camlet cloak as she lay, and the straw had kept her warm. "I'm much obliged to you," she said—"will ye take a—will ye let me give you—"

"No a farden, no a farden," cried the man. "I would convoy ye to Mrs. Macfarlane's door, but I have to supper my horse. Will ye gie me a shake of your hand? You're a bonny lass and I hope ye'll be a guid ane—but mind there's awfu' temptations in thae towns."

Kirsteen walked away very stiff but refreshed, half angry, half amused by this last caution. She said to herself with a blush that he could not have known who she was—a lady! or he would not have given her that warning, which was not applicable to the like of her. They said poor lassies in service, out among strangers, stood in need of it, poor things. It was not a warning that had any meaning to a gentlewoman; but how was the man to know?

She went on still in a strange confusion of weariness and the haze of awakening to where the little town of Arrochar lay low by the banks of the loch. It was dark there sooner than in other places, and already a light or two began to twinkle in the windows.

Two or three men were lingering outside the inn when Kirsteen reached the place, and daunted her—she who was never daunted. She went quickly past, as quickly as her fatigue would admit, as if she knew where she was going. She thought to herself that if any one remarked it would be thought she was going home to her friends, going to some warm and cheerful kent place—and she a waif and outcast on the world! When she had passed, she loitered and looked back, finding a dim corner where nobody could see her, behind the little hedge of a cottage garden. Presently a woman in a widow's cap came briskly out to the door of the little inn, addressing a lively word or two to the loitering men, which made them move and disperse; and now was Kirsteen's time. She hurried back and timidly approached the woman at the inn door as if she had been a princess. "Ye'll maybe be Mistress Macfarlane?" said Kirsteen.

"I'm just that; and what may ye be wanting? Oh, I see you're a traveller," said the brisk landlady; "you'll be wanting lodging for the night."

"If you have a room ye can give me—with a bed—I've had a long walk—from near Loch Fyne," said Kirsteen, feeling that explanation was necessary, and looking wistfully in the face of the woman on whom her very life seemed to depend. For what if she should refuse her, a young girl all alone, and turn her away from the door?

Mrs. Macfarlane was too good a physiognomist for that—but she looked at Kirsteen curiously in the waning light. "That's a far way to come on your feet," she said, "and you're a young lass to be wandering the country by yourself."

"I'm going—to take up a situation," said Kirsteen. "If ye should have a room——"

"Oh, it's no for want of a room. Come in, there's plenty of room. So ye're going to take up a situation? Your minnie must have been sair at heart to let you gang afoot such a weary way."

"There was no other—convenience," said

Kirsteen, sick and faint. She had to make an effort not to cry. She had not thought of this ordeal, and her limbs would scarcely sustain her.

"Come in," said the woman. "Would you rather go to your bed, or sit down by the fire with me? Lord bless us, the poor thing's just fainting, Eelen. Take her into the parlour, and put her in the big chair by the fire."

"I'm not fainting—I'm only so tired I cannot speak," said Kirsteen, with a faint smile.

"Go ben, go ben," said Mrs. Macfarlane, "and I'll make the tea, and ye shall have a cup warm and strong. There's naething will do you so much good."

And to lie back in the big chair by the warm fire seemed like paradise to Kirsteen. This was her fortunate lot on her first night from home.

CHAPTER II.

She had, however, much questioning to go through. There was but little custom to occupy the woman of the inn, and the mingled instincts of kindness and gossip, and that curiosity which is so strong among those who have little to learn save what they can persuade their neighbours to tell them, had much dominion over Mrs. Macfarlane. Kindness perhaps was the strongest quality of all. Her tea was hot and strong and what she considered well "masket" before the fire; and when the Highland maid, who could speak little English, but hung about in silent admiration of the unexpected visitor, who was a new incident in the glen, had "boilt" some eggs, and placed a plate of crisp cakes—the oatcakes which were the habitual bread of Scotland at that period—and another of brown barley scones, upon the table, the mistress herself sat down to encourage her guest to eat.

"There's some fine salt herrings if ye would like that better, or I could soon fry ye a bit of ham. We've baith pork hams and mutton hams in the house. But a fresh boilt egg is just as good as anything, and mair nat'ral to a woman. Ye'll be gaun to Glasco where everybody goes."

"Yes," said Kirsteen, with a doubt in her heart whether it was honest not to add that she was going further on.

"I wonder what they can see in't—a muckle dirty place, with long lums pouring out smoke. I wouldna gie Arrochar for twenty o't."

"I suppose," said Kirsteen, "it's because there is aye plenty doing there."

"I suppose sae. And ye're going to take up a situation? It's no a place I would choose for a young lass, but nae doubt your mother kens what she's doing. Is it a lady's maid place, or to be with bairns, or—I'm sure I beg your pardon! You'll be a governess, I might have seen."

Kirsteen had grown very red at the thought of being taken for a lady's maid, but she said to herself quickly that her pride was misplaced, and that it was the best service any one could do her to think her so. "Oh, no," she said, "I'm not clever enough to be a governess. I'm going—to a mantua-maker's."

"Weel, weel—that's a very genteel trade, and many a puir leddy thankful to get into it," said Mrs. Macfarlane. "I'm doubting you're one yoursel', or else ye have lived with better kind of folk, for ye've real genty ways, and a bonny manner. Take heed to yourself in Glasco, and take up with none of thae young sprigs in offices that think themselves gentlemen. Will ye no take another cup? Weel, and I wouldna wonder ye would be better in your bed than any other place. And how are ye going on in the morning? There's a coach from Eelensburgh, but it's a long walk to get there. If ye like Duncan will get out the gig and drive you. It would be a matter of twelve or maybe fifteen shillings if he couldna get a job back—which is maist unlikely at this time of the year."

With many thanks for the offer Kirsteen tremblingly explained that she could not afford it. "For I will want all my money when I get to Glasgow," she said.

"Weel," said Mrs. Macfarlane, "ye ken your ain affairs best. But there's sturdy beggars on the road, and maybe ye'll wish ye had ta'en my offer before you win there."

Kirsteen thought she never would sleep for the aching of her limbs when she first laid herself down in the hard bed which was all the little Highland inn, or even the best houses in Scotland, afforded in that period. Her mind was silenced by this strange physical inconvenience, so that she was quiescent in spirit and conscious of little except her pangs of fatigue. Youth, however, was stronger than all her pangs, and the influence of the fresh mountain air, though charged with damp, in which she had pursued her journey—and she slept with the perfect abandon and absolute repose of her twenty years, never waking from the time she laid her head upon the pillow until she was awakened by Eelen, the Highland maid, whom she opened her eyes to find standing over her with the same admiring looks as on the previous evening.

"Your hair will be like the red gold and your skin like the white milk," said Eelen; "and its chappit acht, and it's time to be wakening."

Kirsteen did not spring from her bed with her usual alertness, for she was stiff with her first day's travels. But she rose as quickly as was possible, and got down stairs to share the porridge of a weakly member of the family who was indulged in late hours, and had a little cream to tempt her to consume the robust food.

"I would have given ye some tea but

for Jamie," said Mrs. Macfarlane, "maybe he'll take his parritch when he sees you supping yours with sic a good heart."

Though she was thus used as an example Kirsteen took leave of the kind innkeeper with a sense of desolation as if she were once more leaving home.

"'Deed, I just wish ye could bide, and gie the bairns their lessons and please a' body with your pleasant face," the landlady said.

Kirsteen went on her way with a "piece" in her pocket and many good wishes.

It was a bright morning, and the sun, as soon as he had succeeded in rising over the shoulders of the great hills, shone upon Loch Long as upon a burnished mirror, and lit up the path which Kirsteen had to travel with a chequered radiance through the bare branches of the trees, which formed the most intricate network of shadow upon the brown path. The deep herbage and multitudinous roadside plants all wet and glistening, the twinkle of a hundred burns that crossed the road at every step, the sound of the oars upon the rowlocks of a fisherboat upon the loch, the shadows that flew over the hills in swift, instantaneous succession added their charms to the spell of the morning, the freshest and most rapturous of all the aspects of nature. Before long Kirsteen forgot everything, both trouble of body and trouble of mind. The fascination of the morning brightness entered into her heart. In a sunny corner she found a bit of yellow blossom of the wild St. John's wort, that "herb of grace" which secures to the traveller who is so happy as to find it unawares a prosperous day's journey, and in another the rare, delicate star of the Grass of Parnassus. These with a sprig of the "gale," the sweet wild myrtle which covers those hills, made a little bouquet which she fastened in the belt of her spencer with simple pleasure. She hesitated a moment to wear the badge of the Campbells, and then with a fantastic half-amused sentiment reminded herself that if she had become the Lady of Glendochart, as she might have done (though ignorant folk took her for a governess or even a lady's waiting woman) she would have had a right to wear it. Poor Glendochart! It would hurt his feelings to find that she had flown away from her home to escape him. Kirsteen was grieved beyond measure to hurt Glendochart's feelings. She put the gale in her belt with a compunctious thought of her old, kind wooer. But at that moment her young spirit, notwithstanding all its burdens, was transported by the morning and the true delight of the traveller, leaving all that he has known behind him for love of the beautiful and the new. It seemed to Kirsteen that she had never seen the world so lovely nor the sun so warm and sweet before.

She had walked several miles in the delight of these novel sensations and was far down Loch Long side, without a house or sign of habitation nigh, when there suddenly rose from among the bushes of brown withered heather on the slope that skirted the road a man whose appearance did not please Kirsteen. He had his coat-sleeve pinned to his breast as if he had lost an arm, and a forest of wild beard and hair inclosing his face. In these days when the wars of the Peninsula were barely over, and Waterloo approaching, nothing was so likely to excite charitable feelings as the aspect of an old soldier—and the villainous classes of the community who existed then, as now, were not slow to take advantage of it. This man came up to Kirsteen with a professional whine. He gave her a list of battles at which he had been wounded which her knowledge was not enough to see were impossible, though her mind rejected them as too much. But he was an old soldier (she believed) and that was enough to move the easily flowing fountains of charity. No principle on the subject had indeed been invented in those days, and few people refused a handful of meal at the house door, or a penny on the road to the beggar of any degree, far less the soldier who had left the wars with an empty sleeve or a shattered leg. Kirsteen stopped and took her little purse from her pocket and gave him sixpence with a look of sympathy. She thought of the boys all away to the endless Indian wars, and of another besides who might be fighting or losing his arm like this poor man. "And I'm very sorry for ye, and I hope you will win safe home," said Kirsteen passing on. But different feelings came into her mind when she found that she was being followed, and that the man's prayer for "anither saxpence" was being repeated in a rougher and more imperative tone. Kirsteen had a great deal of courage as a girl so often has, whose natural swift impulses have had no check of practical danger. She was not at first afraid. She faced round upon him with a rising colour and bade him be content. "I have given ye all I can give ye," she said, "for I've a long, long journey before me and little siller."

"Ye have money in your purse, my bonny lady, and no half so much to do with it as me."

"If I've money in my purse it's my own money, for my own lawful uses," said Kirsteen.

"Come, come," cried the man, "I'll use nae violence unless ye force me. Gie me the siller."

"I will not give ye a penny," cried Kirsteen. And then there ensued a breathless moment. All the possibilities swept through her mind. If she took to flight he would probably overtake her, and in the meantime might seize her from behind when she could not see what he was doing. She had no staff or stick in her hand but was weighted with her bundle and her cloak. She thought of flinging the latter over his head and thus blinding and embarrassing him to gain a little time, but he was wary and on his guard. She gave a glance towards the boat on the loch, but it was in mid-water, and the bank was high and precipitous. Nowhere else was there a living creature in sight.

"Man," said Kirsteen, "I cannot fight with ye, but I'm not just a weak creature either, and what I have is all I have, and I've a long journey before me—I'll give ye your sixpence if you'll go."

"I'll warrant ye will," said the sturdy beggar, "but I'm a no so great a fuil as I look. Gie me the purse, and I'll let ye go."

"I'll not give ye the purse. If ye'll say a sum and it's within my power I'll give ye that."

"Bring out the bit pursie," said the man, "and we'll see, maybe with a kiss into the bargain," and he drew nearer, with a leer in the eyes that gleamed from among his tangled hair.

"I will fling it into the loch sooner than ye should get it," cried Kirsteen, whose blood was up—"and hold off from me or I'll push you down the brae," she cried, putting down her bundle, and with a long breath of nervous agitation preparing for the assault.

"You're a bold quean though ye look so mim—gie me a pound then and I'll let ye go."

Kirsteen felt that to produce the purse at all was to lose it, and once more calculated all the issues. The man limped a little. She thought that if she plunged down the bank to the loch, steep as it was, her light weight and the habit she had of scrambling down to the linn might help her—and the sound of the falling stones and rustling branches might catch the ear of the fisher on the water, or she might make a spring up upon the hill behind and trust to the tangling roots of the heather to impede her pursuer. In either case she must give up the bundle and her cloak. Oh, if she had but taken Donald and the gig as Mrs. Macfarlane had advised!

"I canna wait a' day till ye've made up your mind. If I have to use violence it's your ain wyte. I'm maist willing to be friendly," he said with another leer pressing upon her. She could feel his breath upon her face. A wild panic seized Kirsteen. She made one spring up the hill before he could seize her. And in a moment her bounding heart all at once became tranquil and she stood still, her terror gone.

For within a few paces of her was a sportsman with his gun, a young man in dark undress tartan scarcely distinguishable from the green and brown of the hillside, walking slowly downwards among the heather bushes. Kirsteen raised her voice a little. She called to her assailant, "Ye can go your way, for here's a gentleman!" with a ring of delight in her voice.

The man clambering after her (he did "hirple" with the right foot, Kirsteen observed with pleasure) suddenly slipped down with an oath, for he too had seen the newcomer, and presently she heard his footsteps on the road hurrying away.

"What is the matter, my bonny lass?" said the sportsman; "are ye having a quarrel with your joe? Where's the impudent fellow? I'll soon bring him to reason if you'll trust yourself to me."

Kirsteen dropped over the bank without reply with a still more hot flush upon her cheeks. She had escaped one danger only to fall into another more alarming. What the country folk had said to her had piqued her pride; but to be treated by a gentleman as if she were a country lass with her joe was more than Kirsteen could bear.

He had sprung down by her side however before she could do more than pick up the bundle and cloak which the tramp had not touched.

"He's a scamp to try to take advantage of you when you're in a lone place like this. Tell me, my bonny lass, where ye are going? I'll see you safe over the hill if you're going my way."

"It is not needful, sir, I thank ye," said Kirsteen. "I'm much obliged to you for appearing as you did. It was a sturdy beggar would have had my purse; he ran at the sight of a gentleman; but I hope there are none but ill-doers need to do that," she added with heightened colour drawing back from his extended hand.

The young man laughed and made a step forward, then stopped and stared, "You are not a country lass," he said. "I've seen you before—where have I seen you before?"

Kirsteen felt herself glow from head to foot with overpowering shame. She remembered if he did not. She had not remarked his looks in the relief which the first sight of him had brought, but now she perceived who it was. It was the very Lord John whose remarks upon the antediluvians had roused her proud resentment at the ball. He did not mistake the flash of recognition, and a recognition which was angry, in her eyes.

"Where have we met?" he said. "You know me, and not I fear very favourably. Whatever I've done I hope you'll let me make peace now."

"There is no peace to make," said Kirsteen. "I'm greatly obliged to you, sir; I can say no more, but I'll be more obliged to you still if you will go your own gait and let me go mine, for I am much pressed for time."

"What! and leave you at the mercy of

the sturdy beggar?" he cried lightly. "This is my gait as well as yours, I'm on my way across Whistlefield down to Roseneath—a long walk. I never thought to have such pleasant company. Come, give me your bundle to carry, and tell me, for I see you know, where we met."

"I can carry my own bundle, sir, and I'll give it to nobody," said Kirsteen.

"What a churl you make me look—a bonny lass by my side over-weighted, and I with nothing but my gun. Give me the cloak then," he said, catching it lightly from her arm. "If you will not tell me where we met tell me where you're going, and I'll see you home."

"My home is not where I am going," said Kirsteen. "Give me back my cloak, my Lord John. It's not for you to carry for me."

"I thought you knew me," he cried. "Now that's an unfair advantage, let me think, was it in the schoolroom at Dalmally?

To be sure! You are the governess. Or was it?—"

He saw that he had made an unlucky hit. Kirsteen's countenance glowed with proud wrath. The governess, and she a Douglas! She snatched the cloak from him and stood at bay. "My father," she cried, "is of as good blood as yours, and though you can scorn at the Scots gentry in your own house you shall not do it on the hill-side. I have yon hill to cross," said the girl with a proud gesture, holding herself as erect as a tower, "going on my own business, and meddling with nobody. So go before, sir, or go after, but if you're a gentleman, as ye have the name, let me pass by myself."

The young man coloured high. He took off his hat and stood aside to let her pass. After all there are arguments which are applicable to a gentleman that cannot be applied to sturdy beggars. But Kirsteen went on her way still more disturbed than by the first meeting. He had not recognized her, but if they should ever meet again he would recognize her. And what would he think when he knew it was Drumcarro's daughter that had met him on the hill-side with her bundle on her arm, and been lightly addressed as a bonny lass. The governess at Dalmally! Hot tears came into Kirsteen's eyes as she made her way across the stretch of moorland which lies between Loch Long and the little Gairloch, that soft and verdant paradise. She walked very quickly neither turning to the right hand nor the left, conscious of the figure following her at a distance. Oh, the governess! She will be a far better person than me, and know a great deal more, thought Kirsteen with keen compunction, me to think so much of myself that am nobody! I wish I was a governess or half so good. I'm a poor vagrant lass, insulted on the road-side, frighted with beggars, scared by gentlemen. Oh, if I had but taken that honest woman's offer of Donald and the gig!

CHAPTER III.

KIRSTEEN passed that night at Helensburgh, or Eelensburgh as everybody called it, and next day arrived at Glasgow a little after noon. She had the address there of a friend of Marg'ret's where she would once again find herself in the serenity of a private house. She seemed to herself to have been living for a long time in public places—in houses where men could come in to drink or any stranger find a shelter, and almost to have known no other life but that of wandering solitude, continual movement, and the consciousness of having no home or refuge to which she belonged. Kirsteen had never made a day's journey in her life before that dreadful morning when she set out in the dark, leaving all that was known and comprehensible behind her. She had never been in an inn, which was to her something of a bad place given over to revellings and dissipation, and profane noise and laughter, the "crackling of thorns under the pot." These ideas modify greatly even with a single night's experience of a quiet shelter and a kind hostess—but she looked forward to the decent woman's house to which Marg'ret's recommendation would admit her, with the longing of a wanderer long launched upon the dreary publicity of a traveller's life, and feeling all the instincts of keen exclusivism, which belonged in those days to poorer Scotch gentry, jarred and offended at every turn. To find the house of Marg'ret's friend was not easy in the great grimy city which was Kirsteen's first experience of a town. The crowded streets and noises confused her altogether at first. Such visions of ugliness and dirt, the squalid look of the high houses, the strange groups, some so rich and well-to-do, some so miserable and wretched, that crowded the pavements, had never entered into her imagination before. They made her sick at heart; and London, people said, was bigger (if that were possible) and no doubt more dreadful still! Oh that it could all turn out a dream from which she might wake to find herself once more by the side of the linn, with the roar of the water, and no sickening clamour of ill tongues in her ear! But already the linn, and the far-off life by its side were away from her as if they had passed centuries ago.

She found the house at last with the help of a ragged laddie upon whose tangled mass of nondescript garments Kirsteen looked with amazement, but who was willing apparently to go to the end of the world for the sixpence which had been saved from the tramp. It was in a large and grimy "land" not far from Glasgow Green, a great block of buildings inhabited by countless families, each of which had some different trace of possession at its special window—clothes hanging to dry, or beds to air, or untidy women and girls lolling out. The common stair, which admitted to all these different apartments, was in a condition which horrified and disgusted the country girl. Her courage almost failed her when she stepped within the black portals, and contemplated the filthy steps upon which children were playing, notwithstanding all its horrors, and down the well of which came sounds of loud talking, calls of women from floor to floor and scraps of conversation maintained at the highest pitch of vigorous lungs. "It's up at the very top," said the urchin who was her guide. Kirsteen's expectations sank lower and lower as she ascended. There were two doors upon each stairhead, and often more than one family inclosed within these subdivisions, all full of curiosity as to the stranger who invaded their grimy world with a clean face and tidy dress. "She'll be some charity leddy seeking pennies for the puir folk." "We hae mair need to get pennies than to give them." "She'll be gaun to see Allison Wabster, the lass that's in a decline." "She'll be a visitor for Justin Macgregor, the proud Hieland besom, that's ower grand for the like of us." These were the pleasant words that accompanied her steps from floor to floor. Kirsteen set it all down to the score of the dreadful town in which every evil thing flourished, and with a sad heart and great discouragement pushed her way to the highest story, which was cleaner than below though all the evil smells rose and poisoned the air which had no outlet. The right-hand door was opened to her hurriedly before she could knock, and an old woman with a large mutch upon her head and a tartan shawl on her shoulders came out to meet her. "Ye'll be the leddy from Loch Fyne," she said with a homely curtsey. "Come ben, my bonny leddy, come ben."

After the purgatory of the stair Kirsteen found herself in a paradise of cleanliness and order, in a little lantern of light and brightness. There were three small rooms—a kitchen, a parlour so called, with a concealed bed which made it fit for the combined purposes of a sleeping and living room, and the bedroom proper into which she was immediately conducted, and which was furnished with a tent-bed, hung with large-patterned chintz, each flower about the size of a warming-pan, and with a clean knitted white quilt which was the pride of Jean Macgregor's heart. There was a concealed bed in this room too, every contrivance being adopted for the increase of accommodation. Perhaps concealed beds are still to be found in the much-divided "lands" in which poor tenants congregate in the poorer parts of Glasgow. They were formed by a sort of closet completely filled by the spars and fittings of a bed, and closed in by a dismal door, thus securing the exclusion of all air from the hidden sleeping-place.

The decent woman, who was Marg'ret's old friend, took Kirsteen's bundle from her hands, and opening it, spread out the contents on the bed.

"I'll just hang them out before the fire to give them air, and take out the creases. And, mem, I hope you'll make yoursel' at home and consider a' here as your ain."

"Did ye know I was coming?" said Kirsteen, surprised.

"Only this morning. I got a scart of the pen from Marg'ret Brown, that is my cousin and a great friend, though I have not seen her this twenty years. She said it was one o' the family, a young leddy that had to travel to London, and no man nor a maid could be spared to gang with her; and I was to see ye into the coach, and take good care of ye; and that I will, my bonny leddy, baith for her sake, and because ye've a kind face of your ain that makes a body fain."

In the relief of this unexpected reception, and after the misery of the approach to it which had sunk Kirsteen's courage, she sat down and cried a little for pleasure. "I am glad ye think I've a kind face, for oh, I have felt just like a reprobate, hating everything I saw," she cried. "It's all so different—so different—from home."

Home had been impossible a few days

ago; it looked like heaven—though a heaven parted from her by an entire lifetime—now.

"Weel," said the old woman, "we canna expect that Glasco, a miserable, black, dirty town as ever was, can be like the Hielands with its bonny hills and its bright sun. But, my honey, if ye let me say sae, there's good and bad in baith places, and Glasco's no so ill as it looks. Will ye lie down and take a bit rest, now you're here—or will I make ye a cup of tea? The broth will not be ready for an hour. If I had kent sooner I would have got ye a chuckie or something mair delicate; but there wasna time."

Kirsteen protested that she neither wanted rest nor tea, and would like the broth which was the natural everyday food, better than anything. She came into the parlour and sat down looking out from the height of her present elevation upon the green below, covered with white patches in the form of various washings which the people near had the privilege of bleaching on the grass. The abundant sweet air so near the crowded and noisy streets, the freedom of that sudden escape from the dark lands and houses, the unlooked-for quiet and cheerful prospect stirred up her spirit. The lassies going about with bare feet, threading their way among the lines of clothes, sprinkling them with sparkling showers of water which dazzled in the sun, awakened the girl's envy as she sat with her hands crossed in her lap. A flock of mill-girls were crossing the green to their work at one of the cotton-factories. They were clothed in petticoats and short gowns, or bedgowns as they are called in England, bound round their waists with a trim white apron. Some of them had tartan shawls upon their shoulders. A number of them were barefooted, but one and all had shining and carefully dressed hair done up in elaborate plaits and braids. Kirsteen's eyes followed them with a sort of envy. They were going to their work, they were carrying on the common tenor of their life, while she sat there arrested in everything.

"I wish," she said, with a sigh, "I had something to do."

"The best thing you can do is just to rest. Ye often do not find the fatigue of a journey," said Mrs. Macgregor, "till it's over. Ye'll be more and more tired as the day goes on, and ye'll sleep fine at night."

With these and similar platitudes the old woman soothed her guest; and Kirsteen soothed her soul as well as she could to quiet, though now when the first pause occurred she felt more and more the eagerness to proceed, the impossibility of stopping short. To cut herself adrift from all the traditions of her life in order to rest in this little parlour, even for a day, and look out upon the bleaching of the clothes, and the mill-girls going to work, had the wildest inappropriateness in it. She seized upon the half-knitted stocking, without which in those days no good housewife was complete, and occupied her hands with that. But towards evening another subject was introduced, which delivered Kirsteen at once from the mild *ennui* of this compulsory pause.

"Ye'll maybe no ken," said the old woman, "that there is one in Glasco that you would like weel to see?"

"One in Glasgow?" Kirsteen looked up with a question in her eyes. "No doubt there is many a one in Glasgow that I would be proud to see; but I cannot think of company nor of what I like when I'm only in this big place for a day."

"It's no that, my bonny leddy. It's one that if you're near sib to the Douglases, and Meg does not say how near ye are, would be real thankfu' just of one glint of your e'e."

"I am near, very near," said Kirsteen, with a hot colour rising over her. She dropped the knitting in her lap, and fixed her eyes upon her companion's face. She had already a premonition who it was of whom she was to hear.

"Puir thing," said Mrs. Macgregor, "she hasna seen one of her own kith and kin this mony a day. She comes to me whiles for news. And she'll sit and smile and say, 'Have ye any news from Marg'ret, Mrs. Macgregor?' never letting on that her heart's just sick for word of her ain kin."

"You are perhaps meaning—Anne," said Kirsteen, scarcely above her breath.

"I'm meaning Mrs. Dr. Dewar," said the old woman. "I think that's her name—the one that marriet and was cast off by her family because he was just a doctor and no a grand gentleman. Oh, missie, that's a hard, hard thing to do! I can understand a great displeasure, and that a difference might be made for a time. But to cut off a daughter—as if she were a fremd person, never to see her or name her name—oh, that's hard, hard! It may be right for the Lord to do it, that kens the heart (though I have nae faith in that), but no for sinful, erring man."

"Mrs. Macgregor," said Kirsteen, "you will remember that it's my—my near relations you are making remarks upon."

"And that's true," said the old lady. "I would say nothing to make ye think less of your nearest and dearest—and that maybe have an authority over ye that Scripture bids ye aye respect. I shouldna have said it; but the other—the poor young leddy—is she no your near relation too?"

Kirsteen had known vaguely that her sister was supposed to be in Glasgow, which was something like an aggravation of her offence: for to live among what Miss Eelen called the fremd in a large town was the sort of unprincipled preference of evil to good which was to be expected from a girl who had married beneath her; but to find herself confronted with Anne was a contingency which had never occurred to her. At home she had thought of her sister with a certain awe mingled with pity. There was something in the banishment, the severance, the complete effacing of her name and image from all the family records, which was very impressive to the imagination, and brought an ache of compassion into the thought of her, which nobody ventured to express. Kirsteen had been very young, too young to offer any judgment independent of her elders upon Anne's case, when she had gone away. But she had cried over her sister's fate often, and wondered in her heart whether they would ever meet, or any amnesty ever be pronounced that would restore poor Anne, at least nominally, to her place in the family. But it had not entered into her mind to suppose that she herself should ever be called upon to decide that question, to say practically, so far as her authority went, whether Anne was to be received or not. She kept gazing at her hostess with a kind of dismay, unable to make any reply. Anne—who had married a man who was not a gentleman, who had run away, leaving the candle dying in the socket. A strong feeling against that family traitor rose up in Kirsteen's breast. She had compromised them all. She had connected the name of the old Douglases, the name of the boys in India, with a name that was no name, that of a common person—a doctor, one that traded upon his education and his skill. There was a short but sharp struggle in her heart. She had run away herself, but it was for a very different reason. All her prejudices, which were strong, and the traditions of her life were against Anne. It was with an effort that she recovered the feeling of sympathy which had been her natural sentiment. "She is my near relation too. But she disobeyed them that she ought to have obeyed."

"Oh, missie, there are ower many of us who do that."

Kirsteen raised her head more proudly than ever. She gave the old woman a keen look of scrutiny. Did she know what she was saying? Anyhow, what did it matter? "But if we do it, we do it for different reasons—not to be happy, as they call it, in a shameful way."

"Oh, shameful—na, na! It's a lawful and honest marriage, and he's a leal and a true man."

"It was shameful to her family," cried Kirsteen doubly determined. "It was forgetting all that was most cherished. I may be sorry for her—" she scarcely was so in the vigour of her opposition—"but I cannot approve her." Kirsteen held her head very high and her mouth closed as if it had been made of iron. She looked no gentle sister but an unyielding judge.

"Weel, weel," said the old woman with a sigh, "it's nae business of mine. I would fain have let her have a glimpse, puir thing, of some one belonging to her; but if it's no to be done it's nane of my affairs, and I needna fash my thoom. We'll say no more about it. There's going to be a bonny sunset if we could but see it. Maybe you would like to take a walk and see a little of the town."

Kirsteen consented, and then drew back, for who could tell that she might not meet some one who would recognize her. Few as were the people she knew, she had met one on the wild hillsides above Loch Long, and there was no telling who might be in Glasgow, a town which was a kind of centre to the world. She sat at the window, and looked out upon the women getting in their clothes from the grass where they had been bleaching, and on all the groups about the green—children playing, bigger lads contending with their footballs. The sky became all aglow with the glory of the winter sunset, then faded into grey, and light began to gleam in the high windows. Day passed, and night, the early, falling, long-continuing night, descended from the skies. Kirsteen sat in the languor of fatigue and in a curious strangeness remote and apart from everything about as in a dream. It was like a dream altogether—the strange little house so near to the skies, the opening of the broad green space underneath and the groups upon it—place and people alike unknown to her, never seen before, altogether unrelated to her former life—yet she herself introduced here as an honoured guest, safe and sheltered, and surrounded by watchful care. But for

Marg'ret she must have fought her way as she could, or sunk into a dreadful obedience. Obedience! that was what she had been blaming her sister for failing in, she who had so failed herself. She sat and turned it over and over in her mind while the light faded out from the sky. The twilight brought softening with it. She began to believe that perhaps there were circumstances extenuating. Anne had been very young, younger than Kirsteen was now, and lonely, for her sisters were still younger than she, without society. And no doubt the man would be kind to her. She said nothing while the afternoon passed, and the tea was put on the table. But afterwards when Mrs. Macgregor was washing the china cups, she asked suddenly, "Would it be possible if a person desired it, to go to that place where the lady you were speaking of, Mrs. Dr.—? If you think she would like to see me I might go."

CHAPTER IV.

IF it was strange to sit at that window looking out over the world unknown, and feel herself an inmate of the little house so different from everything she had ever seen, the guest and companion of the old woman whose very name she had never heard till a few days before, it was still more strange to be in the thronged and noisy streets full of people, more people than Kirsteen had supposed to be in the world, under the glaring of the lights that seemed to her to mock the very day itself, though they were few enough in comparison with the blaze of illumination to which we are now accustomed—going through the strange town in the strange night to see Anne. That was the climax of all the strangeness. Anne, whose name was never named at home, whom everybody remembered all the more intensely because it was forbidden to refer to her. Anne, who had gone away from her father's house in the night leaving the candle flaring out in the socket and the chill wind blowing in through the open door. That scene had always been associated in Kirsteen's mind with her sister's name, and something of the flicker of the dying candle was in the blowing about of the lights along the long range of the Trongate, above that babel of noises and ever shifting phantasmagoria of a great city. She could not make any reply to the old woman who walked beside her, full of stories and talk, pointing out to her a church or a building here and there. Kirsteen went through a little pantomime of attention, looking where she was told to look, but seeing nothing, only a confused panorama of crowded dark outlines and wind-blown lights, and nothing that she could understand.

At length they struck into a long line of

monotonous street where there were no shops and no wayfarers, but some lamps which flickered wildly, more and more like the dying candle. Mrs. Macgregor told her the name of the street, and explained its length and beauty, and how it had been built, and that it was a very genteel street, where some of the bailies and a number of the ministers lived. "The houses are dear," she said, "and no doubt it was a fight for Dr. Dewar to keep up a house in such a genteel place. But they external things are of great consequence to a doctor," she added. Kirsteen was dazed and overawed by the line of the grim houses looming between her and the dark sky, and by the flaring of the wild lights, and the long stretch of darkness which the scanty unavailing lamps did not suffice to make visible. And her heart began to beat violently when her guide stopped at a door which opened invisibly from above at their summons and clanged behind them, and revealed a dark stair with another windy lamp faintly lighting it, a stair in much better order than the dreadful one where Mrs. Macgregor was herself living, but looking like a gloomy cleft in the dark walls. Now that she had come so far, Kirsteen would fain have turned back or delayed the visit to which she seemed to be driven reluctantly by some impulse that was not her own. Was it not an aggavation of her own rebellion that she should thus come secretly to the former rebel, she who had been discarded by the family and shut out from its records? She shrank from the sight of the house in which poor Anne had found refuge, and of the husband who was a common person, not one of their own kind. Drumcarro at his fiercest could not have recoiled more from a common person than his runaway daughter, whose object it was to establish herself with a mantua-maker in London. But Kirsteen felt her own position unspeakably higher than that of her sister.

She followed her companion tremulously into the little dark vestibule. "Oh, ay, the mistress is in: where would she be but in, and hearing the bairns say their bits of lessons?" said an active little maid who admitted them, pointing to the glow of ruddy firelight which proceeded from an inner door. And before she was aware Kirsteen found herself in the midst of a curious and touching scene. She had not heard anything about children, so that the sight so unexpected of two little things seated on the hearth-rug, as she remembered herself to have sat in her early days under Anne's instructions, gave her a little shock of surprise and quick-springing kindness. They were two little roundabout creatures of three and four, with little round rosy faces faintly reddened by the flickering light, which shone in the soft glow, their hair half-flaxen, half-golden. Their chubby hands were crossed in their laps. Their mother knelt in front of them, herself so girlish still, her soft yellow hair matured into brown, her face and figure fuller than of old, teaching them with one hand raised. "Gentle Jesus, meek and mild" she was saying: "Dentle Desus, meet and mild," said the little pupils: "listen to a little child." There was no lamp or candle in the room: nothing but the firelight. The two dark figures in their outdoor dresses stood behind in the shadow, while all the light concentrated in this family group. The mother was so absorbed in her teaching that she continued without noticing their entrance.

"You are not saying it right, Dunny; and Kirsty, my pet, you must try and say it like me—Gentle Jesus."

"Dentle Desus," said the little ones with assured and smiling incorrectness incapable of amendment. Kirsteen saw them through a mist of tears. The name of the baby on the hearth had completed the moving effect of old recollections and of the familiarity of the voice and action of the young mother. The voice had a plaintive tone in it, as so many voices of Scotchwomen have. She stood behind in the background, the rays of the fire taking a hundred prismatic tints as she looked at them through the tears upon her eyelashes. Her heart was entirely melted, forgetful of everything but that this was Anne, the gentle elder sister who had taught her childhood too.

"I have brought a young leddy to see you, Mrs. Dewar," said the old woman. Anne sprang up to her feet at the sound of the voice.

"I did not hear anybody come in," she said. "I was hearing them their hymn to say to their papa to-morrow. Is it you, Mrs. Macgregor? You're kind to come out this cold night. Dunny, tell Janet she must put ye to your bed, for I'm busy with friends."

"Na," said the old lady, "we'll not interrupt. I'm going ben to say a word to Janet mysel'. And she'll no interrupt you putting your bairns to their bed."

She drew Kirsteen forward into the influence of the firelight, and herself left the room, leaving the sisters together. Anne stood for a little gazing curiously at the silent figure. She was puzzled and at a loss; the black silk spencer, the beaver bonnet, were common enough articles of dress, and the big veil that hung like a cloud over Kirsteen's bonnet kept the face in the shade. "Do I know ye?" she said going timidly forward. Then with a cry, "Is it Kirsteen?"

The little children sat still on the hearth-rug with their little fat hands crossed in their laps; they were not concerned by the convulsions that might go on over their heads. They laughed at the glancing firelight and at each other in one of those still moments of babyhood which come now and then in the midst of the most riotous periods; they had wandered off to the edge of the country from whence they came. When the two sisters fell down on their knees by the side of the little ones, the mother showing her treasures, the young aunt making acquaintance with them, the rosy little faces continued to smile serenely upon the tears and suppressed passion. "This is Kirsty that I called after you, Kirsteen." "But oh, ye mean for my mother, Anne?" "Kirsty, me!" said little three-year-old, beating her breast to identify the small person named.

"She's Kistina; I'm Duncan," said the little boy who was a whole year older, but did not generally take the lead in society. "They are like two little birdies in a nest," said Kirsteen; "oh! the bonny little heads like gold—and us never to know."

"Will I send them to Janet, or will ye help me to put them to their bed?" said the proud mother. For a moment she remembered nothing but the delight of exhibiting their little round limbs, their delightful gambols, for so soon as the children rose from that momentary abstraction they became riotous again and filled the room with their "flichterin' noise and glee." "I never light the candles till David comes in," Anne said apologetically. "What do I want with more light? For the bairns are just all I can think of; they will not let me sew my seam, they are just a woman's work at that restless age." She went on with little complaints which were boasts as Kirsteen looked on and wondered at the skilled and careful manipulation of her sister's well-accustomed hands.

The bedroom to which the group was transferred was like the parlour lighted only by the fire, and the washing and undressing proceeded while Anne went on with the conversation, telling how Dunny was "a rude boy," and Kirsty a "very stirring little thing," and "just a handful." "I have enough to do with them, and with making and mending for them, if I had not another thing on my hands," said Anne; "they are just a woman's work." Kirsteen sat and looked on in the ruddy flickering light with strange thoughts. Generally the coming on of motherhood is gradual, and sisters and friends grow into a sort of amateur share in it. But to come suddenly from the image of Anne who had left the house-door open and the candle dying in the socket, to Anne the cheerful mother kissing the rosy limbs and round faces, her pretty hair pulled by the baby hands, her proud little plaints of the boy that was "rude" and the girl that was "very stirring," was the most curious revelation to Kirsteen. It brought a little blush and uneasiness along with affection and pleasure, her shy maidenhood shrinking even while warm sympathy filled her heart.

When the children were in bed, the sisters returned to the parlour, where Kirsteen was installed in the warmest corner by the fire. "Would you like the candles lighted? I aye leave it till David comes home: he says I sit like a hoodie crow in the dark," said Anne. There was a soft tone in her voice which told that David was a theme as sweet to her as the children; but Kirsteen could not bring herself to ask any questions about the doctor who was a common person, and one who had no right ever to have intruded himself into the Douglases' august race. Anne continued for a time to give further details of the children, how they were "a little disposed to take the cold," and about the troubles there had been with their teeth, all happily surmounted, thanks to David's constant care. "If ye ever have little bairns, Kirsteen, ye will know what a comfort it is to have a doctor in the house."

"I don't know about the bairns, but I am sure I never will have the doctor," said Kirsteen in haste and unwarily, not thinking what she said.

"And what for no?" said Anne, holding herself very erect. "Ye speak like an ignorant person, like one of them that has a prejudice against doctors. There's no greater mistake."

"I was meaning no such thing," cried Kirsteen eagerly.

"Well, ye spoke like it," said Anne. "And where would we all be without doctors? It's them that watches over failing folk, and gives back fathers and mothers to their families, and snatches our bonny darlings out of the jaws of death. Eh! if ye knew as much about doctors as I know about them," she cried with a panting breath.

"I am sorry if I said anything that was not ceevil," said Kirsteen; "it was without meaning. Doctors have never done anything for my mother," she added with an impulse of self-justification.

"And whose blame is that? I know what David ordered her—and who ever tried to get it for her? He would have taken her to his own house, and nursed her as if she had been his own mother," cried Anne with heat.

Kirsteen with difficulty suppressed the indignation that rose to her lips. "Him presume to consider my mother as if she were his own!" Kirsteen cried within herself. "He was a bonny one!" And there fell a little silence between the two sisters seated on opposite sides of the fire.

After a while Anne spoke again, hesitating, bending across the lively blaze. "Were ye, maybe, coming," she said with an effort, "to tell me—to bring me a—message?"

Kirsteen saw by the dancing light her sister's eyes full of tears. She had thought she was occupied only by the babies and the changed life, but when she saw the beseeching look in Anne's eyes, the quivering of her mouth, the eager hope that this visit meant an overture of reunion, Kirsteen's heart was sore.

"Alack," she said, "I have no message. I am just like you, Annie. I have left my home and all in it. I'm a wanderer on the face of the earth."

"Kirsteen!" Anne sprang to her sister and clasped her in her arms. "Oh, my bonny woman! Oh, my Kirsty!" She pressed Kirsteen's head to her breast in a rapture of sympathetic feeling. "Oh, I'm sorry and I'm glad. I canna tell ye all my feelings. Have ye brought him with you? Where is he, and who is he, Kirsteen?"

Kirsteen disengaged herself almost roughly and with great though suppressed offence from her sister's arms. "If ye think there is any he in the maitter, ye are greatly mistaken," she said. "If ye think I would take such a step for such a motive."

Anne drew back wounded too. "Ye need not speak so stern—I did it myself, and I would not be the one to blame you. And if there's a better reason I don't know what it is. What reason can a young lass have to leave her hame, except that there's one she likes better, and that she's bid to follow, forsaking her father and mother, in the very Scripture itself."

Mrs. Dr. Dewar returned to her seat—throwing back her head with an indignant sense of the highest warrant for her own conduct. But when she resumed her seat, Anne began to say softly: "I thought you had come to me with maybe a word of kindness. I thought that maybe my mother—was yearning for a sight of me as me for her—and to see my bairns. Oh, it would do her heart good to see the bairns! It would add on years to her life. What are ye all thinking of that ye cannot see that she's dwining and pining for a pleasant house and a cheerful life? David said it before—and he was most willing to be at all the charges—but they would not listen to him, and no doubt it's a great deal worse now."

"If you are meaning my mother, she is no worse," said Kirsteen. "She is just about the same. Robbie has gone away to India like the rest; and she just bore it as well as could be expected. I have not heard," said the girl, feeling the corners of her mouth quiver and a choking in her throat, " how she's borne this."

Both of them had the feeling that their own departure must have affected the invalid more strongly than any other.

" But she has not heard about your children, Anne. She would have said something."

Anne's lips were quivering too. She was much wounded by this assertion. She shook her head. " My mother's no one," she said, " that tells everything—especially what's nearest to her heart. Ye may be sure she knows—but she wouldna maybe be ready to speak of it to young lassies like you."

Kirsteen thought this argument feeble, but she said nothing in reply.

" And so Robbie's away," said Anne. " He was just a bit laddie that I put to his bed like my own. Eh, but time goes fast, when ye hear of them growing up that ye can mind when they were born. I tell David our own will just be men and women before we think." This thought brought a smile to her face, and much softening of the disappointment. "Oh, but I would like my mother to see them!" she said.

Kirsteen reflected a little bitterly that this was all Anne thought of, that her curiosity about her sister had dropped at once, and that the children and the wish that her mother should see them—which was nothing but pride—was all that occupied Anne's thoughts. And there ensued another pause; they sat on either side of the fire with divided hearts, Anne altogether absorbed in her own thoughts of the past and present, of her old girlish life which had been full of small oppressions, and of her present happiness, and the prosperous and elevated position of a woman with a good man and bairns of her own, which was her proud and delightful consciousness, and which only wanted to be seen and recognized by her mother to make it perfect. Kirsteen on her side felt this superiority as an offence. She knew that her mother had "got over" Anne's departure, and was not at all taken up by imaginations concerning her and her possible children—though she could not but recognize the possibility that her own flight might have a much more serious effect, and she sat by her sister's hearth with a jealous, proud sensation of being very lonely, and cut away from everything. She said to herself that it was foolish, nay, wrong to have come, and that it was not for her to have thus encouraged the bringing down of her father's house. There was no such thing she proudly felt in her own case.

Suddenly Anne rose up, and lifting two candlesticks from the mantelpiece placed them on the table, "I hear David's step," she said with a beaming face.

"Then I will just be going," said Kirsteen.

"Why should ye go? Will ye no wait and see my husband? Maybe you think Dr. Dewar is not good enough to have the honour of meeting with the like of you. I can tell you my husband is as well respected as any in Glasgow, and his name is a kent name where the Douglases' was never heard."

"That can scarcely be in Scotland," cried Kirsteen proudly, "not even in Glasgow. Fare ye well, Anne. I'm glad to have seen ye." She paused for a moment with a shake in her voice and added hurriedly, "and the bairns."

"Oh, Kirsteen!" cried Anne rushing to her side, "Oh, Kirsteen, bide! Oh, bide and see him! Ye will never be sorry to have made friends with my man."

"Who is that, Anne," said a voice behind them, "that ye are imploring in such a pitiful tone to bide? Is it some unfriend of mine?"

"No unfriend, Dr. Dewar," said Kirsteen, turning round upon him, "but a stranger that has little to do here."

"It is one of your sisters, Anne!"

"It's Kirsteen," cried Anne with wet eyes. "Oh, David, make her stay."

CHAPTER V.

Dr. Dewar was a man of whose appearance his wife had reason to be proud. None of the long-descended Douglases were equal to him either in physical power or in good looks. He was tall and strong, he had fine hands—a physician's hands full of delicacy yet force, good feet, all the signs that are supposed to represent race—though he was of no family whatever, the son of a shopkeeper, not fit to appear in the same room in which ladies and gentlemen were. Kirsteen had stopped short at sight of him, and there can be no doubt that she had been much surprised. In former times she had indeed seen him as her mother's doctor, but she had scarcely noticed the visitor, who was of no interest to a girl of her age. And his rough country dress had not been imposing like the black suit which now gave dignity and the air of a gentleman which Kirsteen had expected to find entirely wanting in her sister's husband. His somewhat pale face, large featured, rose with a sort of distinction from the ample many-folded white neck-cloth—appropriate title!—which enveloped his throat. He looked at the visitor with good-humoured scrutiny, shading his eyes from the scanty light of the candles. "My wife is so economical about her lights," he said, "that I can never see who is here, though I would fain make myself agreeable to Anne's friends. Certainly, my dear, I will do what is in me to make your sister bide. I would fain hope it is a sign of amity to see ye here to-night, Miss Kirsteen?"

"No," said Kirsteen, "it is not a sign of amity. It was only that I was in Glasgow, and thought I would like to see her—at least," she added, "I will not take to myself a credit I don't deserve. It was Mrs. Macgregor put it into my head."

"Well, well," said Dr. Dewar, "so long as you are here we will not quarrel about how it was. It will have been a great pleasure to Anne to see you. Are the bairns gone to their beds, my dear?"

"They're scarcely sleeping yet," said Anne smiling at her husband with tender triumph. "Go ben," she said putting one of the candlesticks into his hand, "and see them; for I know that's what has brought ye in so soon—not for me but the weans."

"For both," he said pressing her hand like a lover as he took the candle from it. Anne was full of silent exultation, for she had remarked Kirsteen's little start of surprise and noticed that she said nothing more of going away. "Well?" she said eagerly, when he had disappeared.

"Well,"—said Kirsteen, " I never heard that Dr. Dewar was not a very personable man, and well-spoken. It will maybe be best for me to be getting home, before it's very late."

"Will ye no stay, Kirsteen, and break

bread in my house? You might do that and say nothing about it. It would be no harm to hide an innocent thing that was just an act of kindness, when you get home. If I am never to get more from my own family," cried Anne, "but to be banished and disowned as if I were an ill woman, surely a sister that is young and should have some kind thought in her heart, might do that. Ye need say nothing of it when you get home."

"I will maybe never get home more," said Kirsteen overcome at last by the feeling of kindred and the need of sympathy.

"Oh, lassie," cried Anne, "what have ye done? What have ye done?—And where are ye going?—If ye have left your home ye shall bide here. It's my right to take care of you, if ye have nobody else to take care of ye, no Jean Macgregor, though she's very respectable, but me your elder sister. And that will be the first thing David will say."

"I am much obliged to you," said Kirsteen, "but you must not trouble your head about me. I'm going to London—to friends I have there."

"To London!" cried Anne. There was more wonder in her tone than would be expressed now if America had been the girl's destination. "And you have friends there!"

Kirsteen made a lofty sign of assent. She would not risk herself by entering into any explanations. "It's a long journey," she said, "and a person never can tell if they will ever win back. If you are really meaning what you say, and that I will not be in your way nor the doctor's I will thankfully bide and take a cup of tea with ye—for it's not like being among strangers when I can take your hand—and give a kiss to your little bairns before I go."

Anne came quickly across the room and took her sister in her arms, and cried a little upon her shoulder. "I'm real happy," she said sobbing; "ye see the bairns, what darlin's they are—and there never was a better man than my man; but eh! I just yearn sometimes for a sight of home, and my poor mother. If she is weakly, poor body, and cannot stand against the troubles of this world, still she's just my mother, and I would rather have a touch of her hand than all the siller in Glasgow—and eh, what she would give to see the bairns!"

Kirsteen, who was herself very tremulous, here sang in a broken voice, for she too had begun to realize that she might never again see her mother, a snatch of her favourite song:

> "'True loves ye may get many an ane
> But minnie ne'er anither."

"No, I'll not say that," said Anne. "I'll not be so untrue to my true love—but oh, my poor minnie! how is she, Kirsteen? Tell me everything, and about Marg'ret and the laddies and all."

When Dr. Dewar entered he found the two sisters seated close together, clinging to each other, laughing and crying in a breath, over the domestic story which Kirsteen was telling. The sole candle twinkled on the table kindly like a friendly spectator, the fire blazed and crackled cheerfully, the room in the doctor's eyes looked like the home of comfort and happy life. He was pleased that one of Anne's family should see how well off she was. It was the best way he felt sure to bring them to acknowledge her, which was a thing he professed to be wholly indifferent to. But in his heart he was very proud of having married a Douglas, and he would have received any notice from Drumcarro with a joy perhaps more natural to the breeding of his original station than dignified. He felt the superiority of his wife's race in a manner which never occurred to Anne herself, and was more proud of his children on account of the " good Douglas blood " in their veins. " Not that I hold with such nonsense," he would say with a laugh of pretended disdain. " But there are many that do." It was not a very serious weakness, but it was a weakness. His face beamed as he came in : though Kirsteen had said that her presence was not a sign of amity he could not but feel that it was, and a great one. For certainly the laird's opposition must be greatly modified before he would permit his daughter to come here.

"Well," he said, making them both start, "I see I was not wanted to persuade her to bide. I am very glad to see you in my house, Miss Kirsteen. Ye will be able to tell them at home that Anne is not the victim of an ogre in human form, as they must think, but well enough content with her bargain, eh, wifie?" He had come up to them, and touched his wife's cheek caressingly with his hand. "Come, come," he said, "Anne, ye must not greet, but smile at news from home."

"If I am greetin' it's for pleasure," said Anne, "to hear about my mother and all of them and to see my bonny Kirsteen."

"She has grown up a fine girl," said the doctor looking at her with a professional glance and approving the youthful vigour and spirit which were perhaps more conspicuous in Kirsteen than delicacy of form and grace. Her indignation under this inspection may be supposed. She got up hastily freeing herself from Anne's hold.

"I must not be late," she said, "there's Mrs. Macgregor waiting."

"Tell the lass to bring the tea, Anne—if your sister is with friends—"

"I'm telling her that her place is here," cried Anne; "it is no friends, it is just old Jean Macgregor who is very respectable, but not the person for Kirsteen. And we have a spare room," she added with pride. "The doctor will hear of none of your concealed beds or dark closets to sleep in. He insists on having a spare room for a friend. And where is there such a friend as your own sister? We will send Jean to bring your things, Kirsteen."

Kirsteen put a stern negation upon this proposal. "Besides," she said, "it would be no advantage, for I am going on to London without delay."

"To London?" cried the doctor. "That's

a long journey for ye by yourself. Are you really going alone?"

"I'm told," said Kirsteen composedly, "that the guards are very attentive, and that nobody meddles with one that respects herself. I have no fear."

"Well, perhaps there is no fear—not what ye can call fear; for, as you say, a woman is her own best protector, and few men are such fools as to go too far when there's no response. But, my dear young lady, it's a long journey and a weary journey; I wonder that Drumcarro trusted you to go alone; he might have spared a maid, if not a man to go with ye." The doctor's weakness led him to enhance the importance of Drumcarro as if it were a simple matter to send a maid or a man.

"Oh, but Kirsteen says," Anne began, remembering the strange avowal, which she did not at all understand, that her sister had made. Kirsteen took the words out of her mouth.

"It's not as if I were coming back to-day or to-morrow," she said quickly, "and to send any person with me would have been—not possible—I will just keep myself to myself and nobody will harm me."

"I am sure of that," said the doctor cheerfully. "I would not like to be the man that spoke a word displeasing to ye with those eyes of yours. Oh, I'm not complaining; for no doubt ye have heard much harm of me and little good—but ye have given me a look or two, Miss Kirsteen. Does not this speak for me?" he added, raising Anne's face which glowed with pleasure and affection under his touch—"and yon?" pointing to the open door of the room in which the babies slept.

Kirsteen was much confused by this appeal. "It was far from my mind to say anything unceevil," she said, "and in your own house."

"Oh, never mind my own house, it's your house when you're in it. And I would like ye to say whatever comes into your head, for at the end, do what you will, my bonny lass, you and me are bound to be friends. Now come, wifie, and give us our tea."

The dining-room in Dr. Dewar's house was

more dignified than the parlour. It was used as his consulting room in the morning, and Kirsteen was impressed by the large mahogany furniture, the huge sideboard, heavy table, and other substantial articles, things which told of comfort and continuance, not to be lightly lifted about or transferred from one place to another. And nothing could be more kind than the doctor who disarmed her at every turn, and took away every excuse for unfriendliness. After the dreadful experiences of her journey, and the forlorn sense she had of being cut off from everything she cared for, this cordial reception ended by altogether overcoming Kirsteen's prejudices, and the talk became as cheerful over the tea as if the young adventurer had indeed been a visitor, received with delight in her sister's house. She went away at last with the old woman greatly against Anne's will who tried every entreaty and remonstrance in vain. "Surely ye like me better than Jean Macgregor!" she said. "Oh, Kirsteen, it's far from kind—and the spare room at your disposition, and the kindest welcome—I will let you give the bairns their bath in the morning. Ye shall have them as long as you please," she said with the wildest generosity. It was Dr. Dewar himself who interrupted these entreaties.

"My dear," he said, "Kirsteen has a great deal of sense, she knows very well what she's doing. If there is a difficulty arisen at home as I'm led to conclude, it will just make matters worse if she's known to be living here."

"I was not thinking of that," cried Kirsteen, feeling the ungenerosity of her motives.

"It may be well that ye should. I would not have you anger your father, neither would Anne for any pleasure of hers. She is in a different position," said the doctor. "She's a married woman, and her father cannot in the nature of things be her chief object. But Kirsteen, my dear, is but a girl in her father's house, and whatever her heart may say she must not defy him by letting it be known that she's living here. But to-morrow is the Sabbath-day. The coach does not go, even if she were so far left to herself as to wish it; and it could not be ill taken that you should go to the kirk together and spend the day together. And then if ye must go, I will engage a place in the coach for ye and see ye off on Monday morning."

"Oh, I must go, and I almost grudge the Sabbath-day," said Kirsteen. "I am so restless till I'm there. But I must not give you all that trouble."

"It's no trouble. I'll go with ye as far as the coach-office. I wish I was not so busy," said Dr. Dewar with a delightful sense of his own consequence and popularity, and of the good impression it would make. "I would convoy ye to London myself. But a doctor is never at his own disposition," he added, with a shake of his head.

The Sunday which followed was strange yet delightful to Kirsteen. It was like the last day of a sailor on shore before setting forth upon the unknown, but rather of a sailor like Columbus trusting himself absolutely to the sea and the winds, not knowing what awaited him, than the well-guided mariners of modern days with charts for every coast and lighthouses at every turn. Kirsteen looked

> "On land and sea and shore,
> As she might never see them more."

All was strange to her even here, but how much stranger, dark, undeciphered, unknown was that world upon the edge of which she stood, and where there was absolutely nothing to guide her as to what she should encounter! Kirsteen was not quite sure whether she could understand the language which was spoken in London; the ways of the people she was sure she would not understand. Somewhere in the darkness that great city lay as the western world lay before its discoverer. Kirsteen formed an image to herself of something blazing into the night full of incomprehensible voices and things; and she had all the shrinking yet eagerness of a first explorer not knowing what horrors there might be to encounter, but not his faith in everything good. The Sunday came like a strange dream into the midst of this eagerness yet alarm. She was almost impatient of the interruption, yet was happy in it with the strangest troubled happiness; though it was so real it was bewildering too, it was a glimpse of paradise on the edge of the dark, yet unreal in its pleasure as that vast unknown was unreal. She played with the children, and she heard them say their prayers, the two little voices chiming together, the two cherub faces lifted up, while father and mother sat adoring. It was like something she had seen in a dream—where she was herself present, and yet not present, noting what every one did. For up to this time everything had been familiar in her life—there had been no strangeness, no new views of the relationship of events with which she was too well acquainted to have any room for flights of fancy.

And then this moment of pause, this

curious, amusing, beautiful day passed over, and she found herself in the dark of the wintry morning in the street all full of commotion where the coach was preparing to start. She found her brother-in-law (things had changed so that she had actually begun to think of him as her brother-in-law) in waiting for her to put her in her place. Kirsteen's chief sensation in all that crowded, flaring, incomprehensible scene, with the smoky lamps blazing, and the horses pawing and champing, and every one shouting to every one else about, was shame of her bundle and fear lest the well-dressed, carefully-brushed doctor should perceive with what a small provision it was that she was going forth into the unknown. No hope of blinding his eyes with the statement that she was going to friends in London if he saw what her baggage consisted of. He put her, to her surprise, into a comfortable corner in the interior of the coach, covering her up with a shawl which he said Anne had sent. "But I was going on the outside," said Kirsteen.

"Ye canna do that," he said hastily. "You would get your death of cold, besides there was no place." "Then there is more money to pay," she said, feeling for her purse, but with a secret pang, for she was aware how very little money was there. "Nothing at all," he said waving it away, "they are just the same price, or very little difference. Good-bye, Kirsteen, and a good journey to you. A doctor's never at his own disposition." "But the money, I know it's more money." "I have not another moment," cried the doctor darting away. Was it possible that she was in debt to Dr. Dewar? She had almost sprung after him when Mrs. Macgregor appeared carrying the bundle and put it on Kirsteen's knee. "Here is your bundle, Miss Kirsteen; and here's a little snack for you in a basket." Thank heaven he had not seen the bundle, but had he paid money for her? Was she in debt to Anne's husband, that common person? There was no time, however, to protest or send after him. With a clatter upon the stones, as if a house were falling, and a sound on the trumpet like the day of judgment, the coach quivered, moved, and finally got under way.

CHAPTER VI.

It was dark again on the second afternoon when Kirsteen, all dizzy, feverish, and bewildered, attained once more, so to speak, to solid ground, after so much that had flown past her, endless, monotonous whirling in inconceivable flats and levels through night and through day. She put her foot upon the pavement timidly, and gave a frightened glance about her, knowing herself to be in London—that fabulous place of which she had never been sure whether it were not altogether a fairy tale. The journey had been like a dream, but of a different kind. She had seemed to herself to be sitting still as in an island in the seas and seeing the wastes of earth sweep past her, field pursuing field. There were hills too, but little ones, not much worthy the attention, and they too went coursing after each other, with all the sheep upon them and the trees and villages at their feet. There were pauses in the dream in which a great deal of commotion went on, and horses champed, and men shouted, and the coach swayed to and fro; but she formed to herself no definite idea of anything that was going on. People came to the coach door and spoke of dinner and supper, but Kirsteen was too shy to eat, though now and then she stepped down, feeling that she was stiffening into stone. And then the long night came, through which went the same roll and jar and jolt of the coach, and now and then a feverish interval of noise and distraction breaking the doze into which she had fallen. She was too much agitated, too unassured, too conscious of the break with all her former life and habits which she was making to enjoy the journey or the sight of so many new places or the novelty in everything. And yet there was a certain wild pleasure in the rush through the night, even in the languor of weariness that crept over her and betrayed her into sleep, and the strange awakening to feel that it was no dream but that still, even while she slept, the fields and hedges were flying past and the journey going on. The second day, however, was one long bewilderment and confusion to Kirsteen, who was altogether unaccustomed to the kind of fatigue involved in travelling; and when she was set down finally in the midst of all the lights and commotion, the passengers tumbling down from above and from behind, the little crowd of people awaiting their friends, the ostlers, the coachmen, the porters with the luggage, her bewilderment reached its climax. She was pushed about by men running to and fro, getting out boxes and bags and every kind of package, and by the loiterers who had gathered to see the coach come in, and by the people who had not found their friends, some of whom came and peered into her face, as if she might perhaps be the person for whom they looked. Kirsteen at length managed to get out of the crowd, and stood in a corner waiting till the din should be over, observing with all the keenness that was left in her till she found some one whose face she could trust. She found at last a man who was "a decent-like man," whom she thought she could venture to address, and, going up to him, asked if he could direct her to Miss Jean Brown's, the mantua-maker? "I have got the address in my pocket," she said, "but perhaps ye will know." "No, miss," said the decent-like man, "there's a many Browns. I think I knows half a hundred." "She is a person from Ayrshire," said Kirsteen. "They don't put up where they comes from, not commonly," said her friend, with a grin, "but if you 'as a letter, miss, I advise you to look at it." Kirsteen had doubts about betraying the whereabouts of her pocket in this strange place, but another glance assured her that he was an unusually decent-like man; and, besides, what could she do? She took out cautiously the letter with Miss Jean

Brown's address. "Chapel Street, Mayfair, will that be near hand?" she said.

"Bless you, that's the West End, that is—it's miles and miles away."

Kirsteen's heart sank so that she could have cried—miles and miles!—after her long jolting in the coach. The tears came to her eyes. But after a moment she recovered herself, feeling the utter futility of yielding to any weakness now. "Could you direct me the way to go?" she said, "for I'm a stranger in London." To see her standing there, with her bundle in her hand and her cloak on her arm, making this very unnecessary explanation was a pathetic sight. The decent-like man was touched—perhaps he had daughters of his own.

"I might find the way," he said, "for I'm a Londoner born, but a stranger like you, fresh from the country, as anybody can see, and ready to believe whatever is told you—no, no! The thing you've got to do, miss, is to take a coach—"

"A coach!" said Kirsteen in horror. "Is

London such a big place, then, that it wants a coach to go from one part to another?"

"It's a hackney coach, if you have ever heard of such a thing," said the man. "I'll call one for you if you please. It is the best thing to do. You could never find your way by night even though you might in the day."

Kirsteen hesitated for a moment. "It will cost a great deal," she said, looking wistfully from the yard into the crowded street, with its flaring lamps, and the hoarse cries that came from it. She shrank back to the side of her new friend as she gazed, feeling more than ever like a shipwrecked mariner, not knowing among what kind of savages she might fall. "Oh, will ye tell me what to do?" she said, with a quite unjustifiable faith in the decent-like man.

However, it is sometimes good to trust, and the result of Kirsteen's confidence was that she soon found herself in a hackney coach, driving, a very forlorn wayfarer indeed, through what seemed to be an endless succession of streets. She had asked her friend humbly whether he would take it amiss if she offered him a shilling for his kindness, and he had taken a load off her mind by accepting the coin with much readiness, but in return had filled her with confusion by asking where was her luggage? "Oh, it will be quite right when I get there," Kirsteen had said, deeply blushing, and feeling that both the coachman and her acquaintance of the yard must think very poorly of her. And then that long drive began. Every corner that was turned, and there were she thought a hundred, Kirsteen felt that now at last she must have reached her journey's end; and on each such occasion her heart gave a wild throb, for how could she tell how Miss Jean would receive her, or if there would be rest for her at last? And then there would come a respite, another long ramble between lines of dark houses with muffled lights in the windows, and then another corner and another leap of her pulses. She thought hours must have elapsed before at last, with a jar that shook her from head to foot, the lumbering vehicle came to a stop. Kirsteen stepped out almost speechless with excitement and gave something, she could scarcely tell what, to the coachman; and then even this conductor of a moment, whose face she could scarcely see in the dark, clambered up on his box and trotted away, leaving her alone. She thought, with a pang, that he might have waited just a moment to see whether they would let her in. It would only have been kind—and what could she do in that dreadful case if they did not? And what was she to Miss Jean Brown that they should let her in? Her loneliness and helplessness, and the very little thread of possibility that there was between her and despair, came over Kirsteen like a sudden blight as she stood outside the unknown door in the dark street. She began to tremble and shiver, though she tried with all her might to subdue herself. But she was very tired—she had eaten scarcely anything for two days. And this great gloomy town which had swallowed her little existence seemed so dark and terrible. There was no light to show either knocker or bell, and she stood groping, almost ready to give up the attempt and sit down upon the steps and be found dead there, as she had heard poor girls often were in London. She had come to this pitch of desperation when her hand suddenly touched something that proved to be a bell. Immediately her heart stood still, with a new and keener excitement. She waited clinging to the railing, holding her breath.

It seemed a long time before there was any response. Finally a door opened, not the door at which Kirsteen stood, but one below, and a faint light shone out upon a little area into which stepped a figure half visible. "Who is there? And what may you be wanting?" said a voice.

„ I was wanting to speak to Miss Jean Brown," Kirsteen said.

"Miss Brown never sees anybody at this hour. Ye can come to-morrow if ye want to see her."

"Oh," cried Kirsteen, her voice shrill

with trouble, "but I cannot wait till to-morrow! It's very urgent. It's one from her sister in Scotland. Oh, if ye have any peety ask her—just ask her!—for I cannot wait."

Another figure now came out below, and there was a short consultation. "Are ye the new lass from the Hielands?" said another voice.

Even at this forlorn moment the heart of Kirsteen Douglas rose up against this indignity. "I am from the Hielands," she said: then anxiety and wretchedness got the better of her pride. "Yes, yes," she cried, "I am anything ye please; but let me in, oh, let me in, if ye would not have me die!"

"Who is that at the front door? Can ye not open the front door? Is there not a woman in the house that has her hearing but me that am the mistress of it?" cried a new voice within; a vigorous footstep came thumping along the passage, the door was suddenly thrown open, and Kirsteen found herself in front of a flaring candle which dazzled her eyes, held up by a woman in a rustling silk dress half covered by a large white muslin apron. Perhaps the white apron made the most of the resemblance, but the worn-out girl was not in a condition to discriminate. She stumbled into the house without asking another question, and crying "Oh, Miss Jean!" half fell at the feet of Marg'ret's sister, feeling as if all her cares were over and her haven reached.

"Yes, I am just Miss Jean," said the mistress of the house, holding her candle so as to throw its full light on Kirsteen's face. "But who are you? I dinna ken ye. You're from the auld country, that's easy to be seen; but I canna take in every Scots lass that comes with Miss Jean in her mouth. Who are ye, lassie? But ye're no a common lass. The Lord keep us, ye'll never be my sister Marg'ret's young leddy from Drumcarro?"

Miss Jean put down her candle hastily on a table, and took Kirsteen's hands. "You're cauld and you're in a tremble, and ye dinna say a word. Come in, come in to the fire, and tell me, bairn, if it's you."

Then there followed a few moments or minutes in which Kirsteen did not know what happened. But the clouds cleared away and she found herself in a room full of warm firelight, seated in a great chair, and herself saying (as if it was another person), " I thought I had got home and that it was Marg'ret."

" But you called me Miss Jean."

"Ah," said Kirsteen, now fully aware what she was saying and no longer feeling like another person. " I knew it was Miss Jean, but it was my Marg'ret too. It was maybe this," she said, touching the white apron, "but it was mostly your kind, kind eyne."

" I'm feared you're a flatterer," said Miss Jean ; " my eyne might be once worth taking notice of, but not now. But you're just worn out, and famishing, and cauld and tired. Eh, to think a Miss Douglas of Drumcarro should come to my house like this, and nobody to meet you, or receive you, or pay you any attention! It was just an inspiration that I went to the door myself. But your room will be ready in a moment, and ye shall have some supper and a cup of tea." She paused a moment and cast a glance round. "Did you bring your—luggage with ye?" she said.

Kirsteen laughed, but blushed a little. "I have nothing but my bundle; I came away in such a hurry—and on my feet."

Miss Jean blushed far more than Kirsteen did. She "thought shame for the servants." "We must say ye left it at the office and it's coming to-morrow," she said anxiously. And then care and warmth and a sense of well-being and comfort and rest so enveloped Kirsteen that she remembered little more. There was a coming and going of various faces into the light, a bustle of preparation, Miss Jean's keys taken out and brought back, consultations about the spare room, and the well-aired sheets, through all of which she sat happy and passive, seeing and hearing everything once more as if she were another person. The dark seas seemed to have been traversed, the unknown depths fathomed, and paradise attained. Perhaps the blazing fire, the fragrant tea, the little hasty meal, were not very paradisaical elements ; but even these creature comforts acquire a sentiment after a long tedious journey, especially when the tired traveller retains all the quick sensations of youth, and is delivered from the horrible exaggerated terrors of inexperience as well as the mere fatigue of body and soul.

CHAPTER VII.

THE journey over and the end attained! This was the thought that came to Kirsteen's mind as she opened her eyes upon the morning—not so tired, she reflected, as she had been at the inn at Arrochar, at Mrs. Macfarlane's, after her first day's walk. Was that a year ago? she asked herself. The adventures by the way, the long lines of loch and hill, the villages and the silent kirks which had seemed to make her safer whenever she saw them, the great flaring dark image of Glasgow, relieved by the sight of Anne and her babies, and the green with the bleaching, the whirl of the long unbroken journey, rattling, jolting, rolling, hour after hour through day and night—the strange passage in the dark through unknown London, and finally this little room in which she opened her eyes, lying still and closing them again to enjoy the sensation of rest, then opening them to see the yellow fog of the morning like a veil against the two small windows already shrouded by curtains, to which Kirsteen was unaccustomed and which seemed to shut out all air and light— if that could be called light that pressed upon the panes with a yellow solidity just touched by a wintry sun. Were all her journeyings over, and had she reached the new world in which she was to live?

Her bundle had been carefully opened, her linen laid out in a drawer half open to show her where to find it, her second gown hung carefully up, shaken out of its creases by a skilful hand. Miss Jean herself had done this, still "thinking shame for the servants" of the new-comer's scant possessions. It was already known all through the house that a distinguished visitor, Miss Douglas of Drumcarro, had arrived, a visitor of whose name Miss Jean was very proud, though a little mystified by her arrival, and wondering much to know what such a phenomenon as the arrival of a girl of good family unattended in London and at her house might mean. She was proud to give the needed hospitality, but why it should be to her, and not to any of her "grand connections," that Kirsteen had come, mystified the dressmaker. And Marg'ret in her letter had given no explanation; "Miss Kirsteen will tell you everything herself," was all she had said. The seamstresses down below, and the servants still lower down who had mistaken the young lady for a new lass, were all in much excitement discussing the strange event. It was probably some story with love in it, the young women thought, and were all eager for a glimpse of the new-comer or for any contribution to her history.

She was nearly dressed when Miss Jean came with a gentle tap at the door. " I was thinking you would perhaps like your breakfast in bed, my dear young lady. You have had a dreadful journey. From Glasgow in two days and cramped up in the coach the whole time. But bless me, you are already dressed," she added, scanning the gown in which Kirsteen had just clothed herself, from head to foot, or rather from hem to throat. Miss Jean looked it all over, and gave it a twitch here and there, and smoothed the shoulders with her hand. "It's not ill made for the country," she said, "and fits you well enough, but these little puffed sleeves are out of fashion for morning dress. You must let me put you in the mode, Miss Douglas, before ye are seen in the world."

Miss Jean herself wore a stuff gown, crossed over upon the bosom, and open at the neck which was covered with a neckerchief of voluminous white net, underneath the gown. She wore a brown front with little curls, and a close cap tied under her chin for morning wear, with a large and long muslin apron trimmed round with muslin work and lace. She had a large and ruddy countenance with eyes like Marg'ret's, kind and soft. Kirsteen was surprised to find, however, how little in the morning was the resemblance which she had thought so great in the night. Marg'ret, though the virtual mistress of the house at home, never changed the dress and aspect of a servant woman for anything more becoming the housekeeper. But Miss Jean was more imposing than many of the country ladies, with a large gold watch like a small warming-pan hooked to her side, and her handkerchief fastened by a brooch of real pearls. To have this personage addressing her so respectfully, looking forward to her entry into the grand world, overwhelmed the girl who already she felt owed her so much.

"Oh," she said, "Miss Jean—I have not come to London to be seen in the world. I'm just a poor runaway from home. I promised Marg'ret I would tell you everything. Nothing can change the Douglas blood. We have that, but we have little more; and all my father thinks of is to push on the boys and restore the old family. The lassies are just left to shift for themselves."

"That is often the case, my dear young lady. Ye must just marry, and do as well for yourselves in that way."

"We are three of us at home, and we can do nothing, and what does it matter being a Douglas if ye have no siller? I've come away, not to see the world, but to make my fortune, Miss Jean."

Miss Jean threw up her hands in dismay. "Bless the bairn, to make her fortune!" she cried.

"That's just what I intend," cried Kirsteen. "I'll not marry a man to deceive him when I care for nothing but his money. I'll marry no man, except—and I've just come to London to work for my living—and make my fortune, if I can."

"Whisht, whisht, whisht!" cried Miss Jean, "that's all very well in a lad,—and there's just quantities of them goes into the city without a penny and comes out like nabobs in their carriages—but not women, my dear, let alone young lassies like you."

"I will not be a young lass for ever, Miss Jean."

"No," said the dressmaker shaking her head, "ye may be sure of that, my dear lamb. That's just the one thing that never happens. But ye'll be married, and happy, and bairns at your knee, before your youth's past, for that," she said, with a sigh, "I'm thinking, my dear, is the best way. I was never one that had much to do with the men. There's some does it and some not. Look at Marg'ret and me, ne'er had such a thought; but now we're getting old both the one and the other, and who will we have to lay our heads in the grave?—not one belonging to us. We're just as the auld Queen said, dry trees."

"Not Marg'ret," cried Kirsteen, "not while one of us is to the fore! I am not wishing to lay her head in the grave, but for love and faithfulness she will never lack as long as there is a Douglas to the fore."

"It's a real pleasure to me," said Miss Jean, putting her handkerchief to her eyes, "to hear ye speak. And well I know Marg'ret would want before you wanted, any one of the family. So it's on both sides, and a grand thing to see a faithful servant so respected. Now, Miss Douglas—"

"My name is Kirsteen."

"Well, Miss Kirsteen. You'll just take a good rest, and look about you, and see the follies of London before ye think anything more about making your fortune. Eh, to hear those bairns speak! Ye would think it was the easiest thing in the world to make a fortune. Ye would think ye had but to put forth your hand and take it. That's just my nephew John's opinion, that has got a small place in an office in Fleet Street, and is thinking what grand things he'll have in the show the year he's Lord Mayor. He was not satisfied at all with the last one," said Miss Jean with a hearty laugh. "'Auntie,' says he, 'it shall be very different when it comes to my turn.' And the laddie has fifteen shillings a week, and to fend for himself! But, my dear," she said, smoothing Kirsteen's shoulder once more, and giving a twitch to the one line in her gown which did not hang as Miss Jean approved, "by the time we have put ye into the last fashion, and ye've been at a grand party or two, ye'll have changed your tune."

"Who will bid me to grand parties?" said Kirsteen; but Miss Jean had disappeared and did not hear. It gave Kirsteen a little pang to think there was nobody who could interfere, no "grand connections" such as the mantua-maker supposed, to call her to the world, a pang not so much for herself as for the mortification involved in Miss Jean's discovery of the fact. As for grand parties Kirsteen had found out that they were a delusion. The ball at the Castle had filled her with dreams of pleasure, but yet nothing but harm had come of it. She had been neglected while there, and received none of the homage which every girl is taught to expect, and she had found only Glendochart, whose suit had cost her her home and everything that had been dear. A tear stole to Kirsteen's eye as she made this reflection, but it never fell, so quickly did her heart rise to the excitement of the novelty around her. She said to herself that even if there was no Glendochart she would not now go back. She would stay and work and make her fortune, and make Jeanie an heiress, and get every dainty that London could provide to send to her mother. She would buy a carriage for her mother, and easy couches and down pillows and everything that heart could desire; and then when *he* came back— the tear rose again, but only to make brighter the triumphant smile in Kirsteen's eyes. Let the others go to grand parties if they could (Mary would like it) but as for her, she would make her fortune, and be a help to every one that bore her name. She knelt down by her bedside to say her prayers, her heart so throbbing with purpose and anticipation that she could scarcely go through these devout little forms which had been the liturgy of her childhood. "Oh, that I may make my fortune and help them all," was the real petition of her heart. To suggest anything so worldly to her Maker would have been blasphemy according to the creed which Kirsteen had been taught, but this was the breath of intense aspiration that carried up the little innocent petitions. She rose from her knees in a thrill of purpose and feeling. "They shall not be shamed as they think, they shall be thankful there was Kirsteen among the lassies, as well as seven sons to make Drumcarro great again. Oh, maybe not Drumcarro but the old Douglas country!" Kirsteen said to herself. And so went down stairs glowing to see what the new sphere was in which she was to conquer the world. And then when *he* came back!

Kirsteen was quite unacquainted with the kind of house, tall and straight and thin, in which, as in the fashionable quarter, Miss Jean had established herself. The thread of narrow street filled with a foggy smoky air through which the red morning sun struggled—the blank line of houses opposite, and the dreary wall of the church or chapel which gave it its name seemed to her petty and dingy and small beyond description, all the more that Miss Jean evidently expected her visitor to be impressed with the fashionable character of the locality. "The rooms were a great deal bigger where we were, near Russell Square," she said, "and more convenient for the work ; but fashion is just everything, and this is where all my leddies live. You could not be expected to go back to Bloomsbury having once got foot in Mayfair." Naturally Kirsteen was quite incapable of contradicting this axiom, which everybody in the work-room considered incontrovertible. The work-room was a long room built out at the back of the house, with many windows, and walls which had no decoration except a few plates of the fashions pinned to them, as being particularly lovely. A long table ran down the middle at which were seated a number of young women, every one of whom to Kirsteen's inexperienced perceptions was infinitely more fashionable, more imposing than her highest conception of herself had ever come to ; and they spoke fine English, with an accent which was to be sure not so easily understood as her own, but had an air of refinement which impressed Kirsteen much. Were they all gentlewomen, come like herself to make their fortunes? She made a timid question on this subject to Miss Jean which was answered almost indignantly, " Gentlewomen ! Not one of them—havering, glaikit lassies ! " was the reply.

"They speak such fine English," said Kirsteen.

Miss Jean kept her word and took her to see all the " ferlies "—London Bridge, and the Exchange, and the Guildhall, with Gog and Magog guarding the liberties of the city, and to take a walk in the park which was just like the country, and where a glass of new milk warm from the cow was given her as a treat. And she was taken to see the coaches come in with the news from the Continent about Boney's escape and the progress that adventurer was making, and the orders to the troops that were to crush him. Kirsteen thanked God that neither her brother nor *him* were in the King's army, but away in India where, indeed, there was fighting going on continually though nobody knew much about it. And she likewise saw Westminster and St. Paul's, both of which overawed her but did not connect themselves with any idea of worship ; her little kirk at home, and the respectable meeting-house at Glasgow to which she had gone with Anne, being all she knew of in that way. She maintained her composure wonderfully through all these sight-seeings, showing no transport either of admiration or wonder, something to the disappointment of Miss Jean. This was not owing to want of interest, however, but partly to a Scotch shyness of expressing herself, and the strong national objection to demonstration or rhapsodies of any kind—and partly to the high tension in which her mind was —a sort of exaltation which went beyond any tangible object, and even made most things a little disappointing, not so splendid as imagination had suggested. The one thing that did overcome Kirsteen's composure was the extent of the streets, tedious, insignificant, and unlovely but endless, going on and on to the end of all things, and of the crowd, which she did not admire in itself, which was often dirty, noisy, and made her shrink, but which also was endless, abounding everywhere. You left it in Fleet Street only to find it again in Piccadilly, Kirsteen thought, gaping at the coaches before the White Horse Cellar just as it had gaped at her own coach where she arrived, which was, she was told, far away in the city. Where did the people come from? Where did they disappear to? Did they live anywhere or sleep in bed, or were they always about the streets day and night? This was one of the things that made her more indifferent to the sights; for her eyes were always wandering away after the people about whom she did not like to ask questions. She saw the Prince Regent riding out accompanied by his gentlemen, "the grandest gentlemen in the land," Miss Jean explained, telling Kirsteen a name here and there which were completely unknown to the Highland girl—who did not admire her future sovereign. In this way a week passed, Kirsteen vainly attempting to be suffered to do something more than sit in the parlour and read a book (it was the *Ladies' Museum*, a magazine of the time in many volumes, and containing beautiful prints of the fashions, which was the chief literature at Miss Brown's), or walk out whenever business permitted Miss Jean an hour of freedom—which was generally in the morning—to see the sights. One day her patience could bear it no longer: she burst forth—

"Miss Jean, Miss Jean, I would rather see no more ferlies. I take you out and spend your time and give a great deal of trouble when all I want is to learn my work, and put to my hand."

"To make your fortune?" said Miss Jean.

"Perhaps at the end—but to learn first,"

said Kirsteen pausing with a deep passing colour, the colour of pride—" my trade."

"Your trade! What would your father say, good gentleman, if he heard you say such words?—Or your mother, poor lady, that has so little health?"

"I've left both father and mother," cried Kirsteen, "but not to come upon others—and ye cannot tear me from my purpose whatever may be said. There's reasons why I will never go back to Drumcarro, till—I will tell you some day, I cannot now. But I'm here to work and not to be a cumberer of the ground. I want to learn to be a mantua-maker to support myself and help—other folk. Miss Jean, if you will not have me I'll have to ask some other person. I cannot be idle any more."

"Miss Kirsteen, there will be grand connections seeking you out and angry at me that let you have your will—and I will lose customers and make unfriends."

"I have no grand connections," said Kirsteen. "You see for yourself nobody has troubled their heads about me. I'm just as lone as the sparrow on the housetop. I've left my own folk and Marg'ret, and I have nobody but you in the world. Why should ye stop me? When my heart's set upon it nobody can stop me," Kirsteen cried, with a flash of her eyes like the flash in her father's when his blood was up.

"Lord keep us! I can weel believe that to look at you," said Miss Jean.

CHAPTER VIII.

It followed as a matter of course that Kirsteen very soon accomplished her purpose. She took her place in the workroom to the great surprise and partial confusion of the workwomen who did not at first know how to teach the lady who had come among them, her qualities and position much magnified by Miss Jean. Some of them were disposed to be impertinent, some scornful, some to toady the young new comer, who, whatever she might be in herself, was undoubtedly Miss Brown's favourite, and able to procure favours and exemptions for those who were her friends. The standing feud between Scotch and English, and the anger and jealousy with which the richer nation regarded the invasions of the poorer, had not yet fallen into the mild dislike which is all that can be said to subsist nowadays in the way of hostile feeling between the two countries. Fierce jests about the Scotch who came to make their fortune off their richer neighbours, about their clannishness and their canniness, and their poverty and their pride, and still lower and coarser jibes about other supposed peculiarities were then still as current as the popular crows of triumph over the French and other similar antipathies; and Kirsteen's advent was attended by many comments of the kind from the sharp young Londoners to whom her accent and her slower speech, and her red hair and her ladyhood were all objects of derision.

But it was soon found that it was not easy to overcome Miss Kirsteen, which was the name she chose to be called by. "I think no shame of my work, but I will not put my father's name in it, for he is old-fashioned and he would think shame," Kirsteen had said—and Miss Jean approved greatly. "It would never do to let these lassies say that there was a Miss Douglas in the workroom with them." Kirsteen had a shrewd suspicion that the Miss Robinsons and Miss Smiths of the workroom would derive little idea of dignity or superiority from the name of Douglas; but even she was not quite so emancipated as to believe them quite ignorant of its importance. When she discovered from the revelations of a toady that they called her Miss Carrots, or Miss Scotchy behind her back, Kirsteen was angry, but dignified, and took no notice, to the great disappointment of her informant. "I did not choose the colour of my hair," she said with much stateliness, little foreseeing a time to come when red hair should be the admiration of the world. But the young women soon heard that their shafts passed over Kirsteen's head and fell innocuous, which is the most safe and speedy extinguisher of malice. To make covert allusions which the object of them never finds out, and utter jibes that are not even heard by the intended butt of the company is poor sport.

Kirsteen had the safeguard of having a great many things to think of. Her thoughts strayed to her mother who would miss her, for whom perhaps she ought to have suffered everything rather than abandon. But what good would I have been to her if they had married me to Glendochart? she said to herself. And then she would ask herself what Glendochart would do, kind man whom she was wae to disappoint or harm, and how Marg'ret would meet the inquiries addressed to her, how much she would be forced to reveal, how much she could hide. And then her thoughts would fly to Anne, and the two babies on the hearthrug, and the doctor, who, no doubt, was well-looking and well-spoken and kind, and who had taken thought for Kirsteen's comfort in a way she had little title to, considering how many prejudices, not yet by any means dispersed, she entertained against him. After these subjects were exhausted, and sometimes before they were begun, her mind, or rather her heart, would fly to wild, unknown landscapes; dimly-imagined wastes of arid heat, in the midst of which a white encampment, and one there of whom she could follow only the personal image, not knowing what he might be doing nor what was the course of that far-off Indian life. He might be in the midst of a battle while Kirsteen, with her head bent over her work and her needle flying, was thinking of him; or travelling in strange ways, on camels over the desert, or mysterious big elephants. The letters of her brothers had been brief records of their own health and appointments and removals and little more. She knew no details of the life of the East. Her imagination could only trace him vaguely through sunshine and splendours unknown. But with all these varied thoughts to fill her mind it may be imagined that Kirsteen was very little affected by the references to Carrots or to the Scotchies who took the bread out of the mouths of English folks. When she did hear them she took them at first with great good humour. "There are plenty of English folk in Scotland," she said. "I've heard that the ladies'-maids and the bairns'-maids are all from here—to teach the children to knap English, which is a little different, as perhaps ye know, from the way we speak." And as for the Carrots she disposed of that very simply. "At home it is Ginger the bairns cry after me," she said. After a while, when she caught the sound of those recurring words among her many thoughts, she would raise her eyes and send a flash among them which daunted the whisperers. But generally Kirsteen neither noticed nor heard the impertinences of her fellow-workwomen, which was the most effectual check of all.

It may not be thought a very high quality in a heroine, but Kirsteen soon developed a true genius for her craft. She had never forgotten Miss Macnab's little lecture upon the accuracy of outline necessary for the proper composition of a gown—and thus had acquired the first principles almost without knowing it. She followed up this, which is the heart of the matter, by many studies and compositions in which her lively mind found a great deal of pleasure. She was not, perhaps, very intellectual, but she was independent and original, little trained in other people's ideas and full of fancies of her own, which, to my thinking, is the most delightful of characteristics. I remember that Mr. Charles Reade has endowed one of the most charming women whom he has introduced to the knowledge of the world with the same gift. Mrs. Lucy Dodd only, I think, made and invented mantles; but Kirsteen tried her active young powers upon everything, being impatient of sameness and monotony, and bent upon securing a difference, an individual touch in every different variety of costume. She was delighted with the beautiful materials, which were thrown about in the work-room, the ordinary mantua-maker having little feeling for them except in view of their cost at so much a yard. But Kirsteen, quite unused to beautiful manufactured things, admired them all, and found a pleasure in heaping together and contrasting with each other the soft silken stuffs, many of them with a sheen of two blended colours called "shot" in those days. Manufactures had not come to such perfection then as now, but there were no adulterated silks or cheap imitations; the very muslins, sprigged and spotted with many fanciful variations, were as costly as brocade nowadays—the kind of brocade which the later nineteenth century indulges in. To be sure, on the other hand, the plain straight gown required very much less material than is necessary now.

I do not myself think that dress was pretty in those days—but every fashion is beautiful to its time. And how the ladies of the early century managed to make themselves comfortable in white muslin gowns in December, even with a cloth pelisse over them, is more than I can divine, though I find in Miss Jean Brown's copy of the *Ladies' Museum* that this was the case. However that may be—and I do not suppose that Kirsteen was before her time, or more enlightened than the rest of the world—it is certain that she applied herself to the invention of pretty confections and modifications of the fashions with much of the genuine enjoyment which attends an artist in all crafts, and liked to handle and drape the pretty materials and to adapt them to this and that pretty wearer, as a painter likes to arrange and study the more subtle harmonies of light and shade. Miss Jean, who had herself been very successful in her day, but was no longer quite so quick to catch the value of a tint, or so much disposed to stand over a subject and attain perfection in the outline of a skirt, was wise enough to perceive the gifts of her young assistant, and soon began to require her presence in the showroom, to consult with her over special toilettes and how to secure special effects. She did this at first, however, with some reluctance, always haunted by the fear that Kirsteen might thus be exposed to remark, and even that she herself might suffer for her audacity in employing a gentlewoman in so exalted a rank of life. "What if some of your grand connections or acquaintances should see ye?" she said. "I have no grand connections," said Kirsteen, vexed to have this want brought back and back upon her consciousness. "For ye see I have all the nobility coming about the place," said Miss Jean proudly; "and now that the season has begun it is different from the winter." "I know nothing about the nobility," cried Kirsteen again. She was angered at last by the assumption, all the more that her want of acquaintance with what was so clearly understood to be her own class, now became so evident to her as to be a grievance—a grievance that she had never been conscious of before.

It happened one day, however, that there came into the show-room, while Kirsteen was there, a very distinguished party indeed, which Miss Jean advanced to the door to meet curtseying to the ground, and which consisted of a large and imposing mother, a beautiful, tall girl, at sight of whom Kirsteen precipitately retired into a corner, and a young gentleman whom in her surprise she did not notice. It appeared, however, that this was not at all the case with him. He glanced round with a yawn as a young man in compulsory attendance on his mother and sister may be excused for doing, then, observing a young figure in the corner, began to take instant measures to discover whether there might not be something here to amuse himself with while the ladies were occupied with their dressmaker. Now it is not easy for a young person in a mantua-maker's show-room persistently to keep her back turned upon a party of customers, and Kirsteen, to give herself a countenance, began to arrange carefully the draping of a piece of silk over a stand, so as to appear to be very much occupied and absorbed in her occupation. That it should really happen to her after all to find a grand acquaintance among Miss Jean's nobility! The discovery was painful yet gave her a certain gratification, for at least to be able to say to Miss Jean that she must run away when the Duchess came in was something, and vindicated her gentility.

On the other hand she said to herself with a little bitterness that most likely they would look her in the face, even Lady Chatty, and never know that they had seen her before.

The young man all this time kept roaming about, looking, as it appeared, at the mantles and the bonnets, but aiming at the stand where Kirsteen, bending over her silk, was pinching and twisting it so as to show its full perfection. He said "Oh!" with a start, when he got into a position in which he could obtain a glimpse of the half-hidden face. She looked up in the surprise of the moment; and there stood the critic of the ball, the sportsman of Loch Long side, he who had been of so much service to her yet had affronted her more than the tramp, Lord John himself—with a delighted smile and mischievous air of satisfaction. "Ho, ho! my pretty maiden—so this was where you were going?" he said to her in a low tone—" I am delighted to see you again."

The colour rushed to Kirsteen's face. She looked up at him defiantly for a moment;

then feeling that discretion was the better part of valour, edged away from where he was standing, bending over her draperies again and drawing the stand softly after her. But Lord John was not to be so easily daunted.

"You can't dismiss me again in that grand style," he said. "Loch Long is one thing and a milliner's in London quite another. Do you think I will believe that you have come here for nothing but to fit gowns on women not half so pretty as yourself?"

Angry words rushed to Kirsteen's lips in a flood—angry, scornful, defiant words, full of contempt and indignation. She was deeply indignant at this attempt to take advantage of what he thought her weakness; but she knew that she was not weak, which is a consciousness that gives courage. Had she been one of the other girls in the workroom to be flattered or frightened or compromised no doubt she would have done some imprudence, implored his silence, or committed herself in some other way. But Kirsteen was out of the range of such dangers. She turned from the stand she had been draping to another piece of work without any visible sign of the disturbance in her mind, and made no reply.

Lord John was not to be shaken off so easily. The time had no very high standard either of morals or manners, and to seize the opportunity of speaking to a pretty girl wherever he found her, was rather expected from, than disapproved in a young man. These were the days in which it was still a civility on the part of a gallant to kiss a pretty maid-servant as he gave her half-a-crown. And milliners were supposed very fair game. He followed her as she opened with much show of zeal a box of French flowers. "Come," he said, "I must choose some of these; I must buy something of you. You'll find me an excellent customer. Choose the prettiest for me, and I'll give you whatever you ask for them. If I had but known when we met last that you were coming here!"

"Miss Kirsteen," said Miss Jean, who had somehow an eye about her to observe what was going on behind. "Will ye please to bring me that new box of French flowers?"

It was a relief yet a new alarm. Kirsteen lifted the light box, and came slowly towards the group. Now it would be seen that they had no more recollection of her than if she had been a stock or a stone. The Duchess did not turn round, but Lady Chatty, conscious of the presence of another girl, and also perhaps vaguely aware that her brother had already found an interest in the opposite corner, looked straight at Miss Jean's new assistant. She gave a start, and clasped her hands; then crying out, "It is Kirsteen!" darted upon her, throwing the box with all the beautiful new French flowers to the ground.

"Oh, dear me, how clumsy I am! Oh, I hope the flowers will take no harm! But it is Kirsteen. Mamma, do you see? Kirsteen Douglas from our own country. Oh, I'm so glad to see you," cried Lady Chatty, seizing her by both the hands out of which her lively onslaught had thrown the box. "You're like a breath of Highland air, you're like the heather on the hills."

And indeed it was a good metaphor as Kirsteen stood confused, with her russet locks a little ruffled as their manner was, and her hazel eyes glowing and her bright face confused between pleasure and vexation and shame.

"It is true that it is me, Lady Chatty," she said, "but you should not have made me let fall the flowers."

"I will help you to pick them up," said the young lady; and Lord John, taking a long step forward as if his attention had been suddenly roused, said, "Can I be of use? I'll help too."

Meantime her Grace, who had turned round at Lady Chatty's cry, stood for a moment surprised, regarding the group all kneeling on the floor, picking up the flowers, and then turned back to have a colloquy with Miss Jean, in which the words "Drumcarro's daughter," and "Glendochart," and "a wilful girl," and "a good marriage," and Miss Jean's deprecating explanation, " I told her so. I told her so, your Grace, but she would not listen to me," came to Kirsteen's ears in her anxiety, while she eluded the touch of Lord John's hand, and tried to respond to all Lady Chatty's eager questions. "Oh, Kirsteen, you should hear what Miss Eelen says of you," said Lady Chatty, "and poor old Glendochart, who is such a nice old man. Why were you so unkind? But I would not marry an old gentleman myself, not if he were a royal duke," cried the girl, raising her voice a little not without intention. "And how clever it was of you to think of coming here! Nobody would ever have found you here if mamma had not taken it into her head to come to Miss Jean's to-day. But oh, Kirsteen, it is a pity, for they will send you home again. I am glad to have seen you, but I am sorry, for mamma is coming to talk seriously to you. I can see it in her face. And papa will hear of it, and he will think it his duty to take an interest. And between them they will make you go home again. And when once they get you back, they will marry you to old Glendochart, whether you like or not!"

CHAPTER IX.

AND indeed the Duchess did come forward with the gravest looks, after the flowers had all been gathered up and restored to the box and her talk was over with Miss Jean.

"Miss Douglas," she said, "I am much surprised to find you here."

"Your Grace," said Kirsteen, "I am very well here."

"That is just your silly notion. A young person of your age is not fitted to dispose of her own life. Your worthy parents had looked out a most suitable match for you, and I cannot but say it was very wrong and a shame to all belonging to you that you should run away."

"I would rather say nothing about it,

madam," said Kirsteen. "Whether that was the cause or not, the heart knoweth its own bitterness; and every one of us, however small we may be, understands their own affairs best."

"No, young lady," said the Duchess, "that's not so. You are not at an age when you are fit to judge. It is just nothing but childish folly," she added, raising her voice also intentionally, and casting a glance towards her daughter, "to object to a good man and a gentleman of a good family, and who is hale and hearty and full of sense—because he is not just as young as some long-legged fool that you may think better worth your pains."

"Like me, for instance," said Lord John in an audible aside.

Her Grace's eyes softened as her look rested for a moment upon her scapegrace. Then she turned back to Kirsteen with her severest look. "It is a very bad example to other foolish young creatures that you have set in running away. But I hope you will think better of it, and be persuaded, and go back to your family," she said.

"I do not think I can do that," said Kirsteen, "for there's nothing changed that I know, and the reason that brought me away is still there."

"Miss Douglas," said the Duchess, "his Grace himself has heard all about this from one and another, and I make little doubt that when he hears where you are and that we have seen you, and what an unsuitable place you are in for a gentleman's daughter, he will take it into his own hands, and just insist that you must go back."

Kirsteen had been standing in a respectful attitude listening to the great lady, answering for herself, it is true, with much steadiness, but also with deference and humility. She raised her head now, however, and looked the Duchess in the face. "I am meaning no disrespect," she said, "but, madam, I am not his Grace's clanswoman, that he should insist. The Douglases I have always heard tell were sovran in their own place, and gave no reverence to one of another name."

"Young lady," cried the Duchess astonished, "you are a very bold person to speak of his Grace in that tone."

"I am meaning no disrespect," Kirsteen said. But she stood so firm, and met her Grace's eye with so little shrinking, that even the Duchess herself was embarrassed. It is unwise to profess an intention of interfering and setting everything straight before you have ascertained that your impulse will be obeyed. The great lady coloured a little and felt herself worsted. It was only natural that she should lose her temper; she turned upon Miss Jean, who stood by very tremulous, half sympathizing with Kirsteen, half overawed by her visitor.

"Then, Miss Brown," she said, "it should be your duty to interfere. It ill becomes you, a person so well supported by the Scots gentry, to back up a young girl of family in rebellion against her own kith and kin."

Miss Jean was much taken by surprise,

yet she was not unequal to the occasion. "I have told Miss Kirsteen," she said, "on several occasions that this was what would happen; that her grand friends would step in, and that we would all be called to account. I hope your Grace will excuse me, but I cannot say more. I have no authority. If your Grace cannot move her, how will she heed the like of me?"

"She is a very self-willed young person," said the Duchess; "but I will see that her friends are communicated with, and no doubt her father will send some one to fetch her away. We will just leave the other question till another time. Charlotte, come away."

"But I must have my gown, mamma," cried Lady Chatty; "indeed I'm not going without my gown. What should I do with all the balls coming on, and nothing to wear? You can go away if you please and send the carriage back for me, or John will take me home. But if all the world were falling to pieces, I must have my gown. You must know, Miss Jean, it is for the birthday, and

I must have something of your very best. Kirsteen, what is the prettiest thing she has? for you must know. I want some of that silver gauze that is like a mist, and I have it in my head exactly how I want it made. Oh, mamma, don't stand and look so glum, but just go away, please, and send the carriage back for me."

The Duchess hesitated for a moment, but in the end took her daughter's advice, as was her custom. "You will not forget, Miss Jean, what I have said. And as for you, young lady, I hope you will reflect upon your position and take the proper steps to put things right," she said severely. "John, you will give me your arm down stairs. And see that you are ready, Charlotte, in a quarter of an hour, when the carriage comes back."

With these words the Duchess went away She could not stand against her beautiful daughter and the necessity of the new gown, but she would not sanction in her own person the example of rebellion and self-assertion. "You will come back for Chatty," she said to her son, relaxing a little when she got outside that home of insubordination. "She is far too free with common people; and that young woman is a very bold-looking person and not society for your sister."

"She is a very pretty person," said Lord John; "I could not think where I had seen her before."

"Pretty! with that red hair!" cried his mother, shaking her head as she got into her carriage and drove away.

"Now, Kirsteen," cried Lady Chatty, "quick, quick, now that mamma's gone—her bark is a great deal worse than her bite—tell me all about it. They wanted to make you marry old Glendochart? Oh, parents are like that everywhere—they want me, too. And couldn't you just face them and get over them as I do? Couldn't you just? Miss Jean, she is crying—but I meant no harm."

"Lady Chatty," said Kirsteen, "will you try and get her Grace not to write? If I were ever so willing my father would never more let me come back. Oh, if I might just be left alone!—for I cannot tell you everything. My family is not like other families. If I was dying for it they would never more take me home again. Oh, if I might just be let alone!"

"I told you, Miss Kirsteen, what would be the end of it," said Miss Jean, "and that you would bring me into trouble too."

"Oh, never mind these old people, they are all the same," cried Lady Chatty. "But," she added, "I almost wonder after all, Kirsteen, you did not marry old Glendochart; he would have freed you from all the rest, and he would have done whatever you pleased. And nobody could have put a question or said a word. So long," said this experienced young lady, looking in Kirsteen's face, "as there was not some one else. Oh, but I see!" she cried, clapping her hands, "there is some one else."

"Will your leddyship look at this?—it is the gauze ye were inquiring after," said Miss Jean. "I will just put it about you over your shoulder, and you will see the effect. And

Miss Kirsteen, who has wonderful taste, will give us her advice. Look now in the cheval glass. What does your ladyship think of that?"

"It's divine," cried Lady Chatty, clapping her hands; and interesting though the other subject was, the new gown and its possibilities, and a delightful discussion as to certain novel effects, carried the day. Miss Jean threw herself ecstatically into Lady Chatty's devices by way of changing the subject, and finally in a whirlwind of questions and suggestions, petitions for Kirsteen's confidence and recommendations of silver trimmings, the visitor was got away at last. Miss Jean, when she was gone, threw the silvery stuff with some impatience upon the floor.

"I have humoured all her whims just to get you clear of her," she said. "Oh, Miss Kirsteen, did I not tell ye what would happen when you were discovered by your grand friends?"

Curiously enough, however, even to Kirsteen's own mind there was a certain solace in the thought that these very great people, who knew so little about her, thought her of sufficient importance to interfere personally in her affairs. Her trouble and confusion before the Duchess's reproof was wonderfully modified by the soothing sense of this distinction. It had been humbling to feel that she had no grand connections, nobody that could interfere. There was consolation in the fulfilment of Miss Jean's prophecy.

And it may be imagined what excitement ran through the house from the garret to the basement some days after when the Scotch maid came into the workroom breathless, with the thrilling news that my lord Duke was in the parlour waiting to see Miss Douglas. His Grace himself! "Lord bless us!" cried Miss Jean, "ye must go down quick, for a great person's time is precious, and I will come myself just when I think the interview's over, for no doubt he will want to give his directions to me." All the needles in the workroom stopped with the excitement of this visit, and the boldest held her breath.

A Duke, no less, to see Miss Carrots, the Scotchy with the red hair! "But that's how they do, they all hangs together," was the comment afterwards, couched in less perfect language perhaps than the supposed pure English which Kirsteen admired. Kirsteen herself rose, very pale yet very determined, from her seat at the long table, and brushed from her dress the fragments of thread and scraps of silk. She said nothing, but walked away to this alarming interview with her heart thumping in her breast, though externally all seemed calm. Kirsteen had a strong inclination to run away once again and be no more seen, when she reached the parlour door; and it was chiefly pride that supported her through the ordeal. She went in with much internal trembling but a pale resolution which no duke nor other potentate could break down.

He was standing playing with his eyeglass against the window, blocking out most of the light—a large man enveloped in the huge folds of his neckcloth, and in layer upon layer of waistcoats, enormous at the shoulders but dwindling towards the legs in tight pantaloons. Truth to tell, his Grace was more nervous, so far as appearances went, than the little girl whom he had been sent to bring to a sense of her duty. He said, "How d'ye do?" very ceremoniously, and offered her a chair. "You're one of our county neighbours, Miss Douglas, I hear. My land marches with Drumcarro, perhaps you will know. It is on the edge of the old Douglas country, which, as luck will have it, now chiefly belongs to me, though it is no doing of mine."

"But my father represents the old Douglases, your Grace, though we have so little of the land."

"It is a long time since," said the Duke, "but it is perhaps true; and you have a right to stand up for your own side. The more reason for the Duchess's great concern at finding you here."

"I am very well here, my lord Duke," said Kirsteen rigidly; she had to keep so much control upon herself not to tremble that she had become as stiff as a wooden image, and was well aware of the fact, which did not add to her comfort.

"You are not my clanswoman, Miss Douglas," said his Grace, using her own expression, "and you know as well as I do I have no power over you. But I think I am perhaps implicated in what has happened from the foolish mistake I made in taking you for the daughter of Glendochart on the occasion when we had the pleasure of seeing you at the Castle. You may have thought from that that he was considered an old man, but he is nothing of the sort. He is younger than I am," said the Duke, waving his hand with an air of conscious youth; "he is a man in the prime of life. As for assuming you to be his daughter, it was only a foolish jest, my dear young lady. For I knew he had no daughter nor child of any kind, being an unmarried man. I hope this explanation will smooth matters," the Duke said, with a demonstrative wave of his hand.

"Oh, it never was that," cried Kirsteen, "it never was that! And I have never said a word about Glendochart, nor given that as my reason. I had other reasons," she said.

"My dear young lady, however you explain it, it was very foolish," said his Grace, "for all you needed to have done was to have said a word to Glendochart himself. He would never have had pressure put upon you. He is as true a gentleman as you will find between this and him. He would never have taken a bride by force. A word to him would have been enough."

"I know that well," said Kirsteen, "oh, I know that well." She added, "But if it please your Grace, I never said it was because of Glendochart. I had—other reasons."

"Oh, you had other reasons?" said the Duke, perplexed. "But I hope now that we have talked it over you will see what is suitable, and just go quietly home."

Kirsteen made no reply.

"I feel convinced," said the Duke, "that

though you may be a little headstrong, you are not just a rebel, liking your freedom, as the Duchess was disposed to think; and now that I have set it all before you, you will just take your foot in hand, as we say in Scotland, and go cannily home."

"I cannot do that, your Grace," said Kirsteen.

"And why cannot you do that? You may depend upon it, it is the only right way. 'Children, obey your parents,' is the word of Scripture. You must really go home. Your forbears and mine have known each other when the Douglases were more on a level perhaps with my family than they are now, so you see I have a certain right to speak. My dear young lady, you will just come home."

"I cannot do that, my lord Duke."

"Hush, hush, ye will allow I must know better from my position and all that. Pack up your things, and I will see that you have a postchaise ready and a servant to take care of you. You see we take a great interest in you, both the Duchess and myself."

"I am much obliged to your Grace—and to the Duchess—"

"Yes, yes; but that's nothing. I will tell somebody to order the postchaise for you, and you'll find, with a little judgment, that all will go well."

He patted her arm softly, stroking her down as if she had been a cat or a child. "Just go cannily home," he said, "that's always the best place for a girl—just go cannily home."

At this moment Miss Jean, unable to contain herself longer, tapped at the door, and Kirsteen made her escape, leaving these high powers to concert the method of her going—a futile proceeding so long as the will of the proposed traveller remained unchanged.

CHAPTER X.

In view of this important reservation, the arrangements made and sanctioned by Duke and Duchess, and feebly but faithfully supported by Miss Jean—who had become fully sensible of the value to herself of Kirsteen's services, yet could not but back up the higher authorities—did not come to very much. Passive resistance is a great power, and even when a child says " I will not," it is policy on the part of his superiors to be quite sure of their power either to convince or coerce before entering upon any controversy. Kirsteen stood quite firm.

" No, my lord Duke, I cannot go home," she said, with a courtesy so respectful that his Grace could only take refuge in the recollection that she was not his clanswoman.

"If ye had been of my name I would not have taken a denial," he said.

"And she would have been of your name if she had married Glendochart," cried the Duchess exasperated.

But Kirsteen stood firm. She would hear of no postchaise. She did not repeat what had been wrung out of her in the first assault that her father would never again receive into his house the fugitive who had escaped from it. Kirsteen had been very well aware of this fact, however, from the beginning, and in her soul it supported her, like a rock to which she had set her back. Her own heart might fail. It did fail often when she thought of her mother. Sometimes she would start up in the night with a wailing cry for Kirsteen ringing in her ears; and at these moments it would seem to her that to set out at once with no easements of a postchaise, but on foot like a pilgrim, guilty of treason to the first love of life, was the only thing for her to do. But these compunctions of affection died away before the recollection of her father's lowering face and the fire in his fierce eyes. She had known it when she stole forth in the dark that miserable morning, escaping from all the limitations of her youthful life. Had there been more time to think, had there not been the terror upon her of his summary and unhesitating tyranny, some other way might have been found. But having once taken such a step Kirsteen knew that no way remained of going back. Like Anne she would be already swept out of the record of the family. No one would be permitted to name her name. And even her mother who wanted her most, would weep, and acquiesce, and find comfort in an additional plaint. Kirsteen was profoundly acquainted with that prosaic course of common life which closes over all events in such a family as her own. It would be like a stone in the water with ever widening, ever fainter circles; and then the surface would become smooth again. It had been so in the case of Anne. She remembered well enough the awed and desolate sensation of the moment, the story about the candle dying in the socket, and the cold wind blowing through the house from the open door; and then a little blank of vacancy, and terror of the forbidden name which would come to their lips unawares; and then,—forgetfulness. Kirsteen knew that the same process would take place in her own case; the father's ban—forbidding that she should be called a child of his or her name mentioned in his house, and the mother's sob, but consent. No romantic superstitions about a father's curse were in Kirsteen's mind. It roused her only to self-assertion, to something of a kindred pride and wrath, and resistance; nor did the thought of her mother's acquiescence in the sentence wound her. Poor mother! The girl was glad to think that there would be no secret struggle in the ailing woman's soul, but only a few tears and all over. Kirsteen had the steadying force of experience to subdue all exaggerated feelings in her own bosom. She knew exactly how it would be. But she knew at the same time that the sentence she had herself called forth was fixed and would not be changed.

And to speak the truth Kirsteen felt the activity and occupations of the new life to be much more congenial to her own energetic and capable spirit than the dull quiet of the old, in which there was no outlet. That she should be seized with a yearning now and then for the sound of the linn, for the silence of the hills, for the wholesome smell of the peats in the clear blue Highland air, was as natural as that she should hear that wail for Kirsteen in the midst of her dreams. These longings gradually built up in her mind an ideal picture of the beauty and perfection of nature as embodied in her own glen, such as is a stay and refreshment to many a heart in the midst of alien life—to many a heart which perhaps in presence of that glen not idealized would be unconscious of any beauty in nature. The glen, and her mother, and little Jeanie—the time would come when she would shower secret gifts and comforts upon all—when they should find out what Kirsteen was by the good things that would come from her—the things soft, and lovely, and comforting, and sweet, which Marg'ret would convey and the father never find out. Go back! Oh, no; she would not if she could go back, and she could not if she would. So what did it matter what Duke or Duchess might say? The postchaise remained unordered; the girl courtesyed to his Grace and her Grace, and stood firm. And by and by that power came in which is of such force in all human things. Duchess and Duke, and Miss Jean, and even Kirsteen herself, carried on by the tide of daily life with its ever new occurrences—forgot; and the little world about settled down calmly as if the present state of affairs was that which had always been.

Some time, however, after these events a significant incident occurred in the history of Miss Jean Brown's mantua-making establishment. A carriage, unknown as yet with liveries and devices which never had appeared before, appeared in Chapel Street and set down a little party of ladies at Miss Jean's door. She advanced to meet them, as was her wont, to the door of the show-room, with a courtesy which would have done no discredit to a queen's drawing-room. But the ladies made a pause, and whispered together, and then the eldest said—"Oh, it is Miss Douglas we want. We wish to give our orders to Miss Douglas. We have never been here before. And it is Miss Douglas we want to see."

Miss Jean, surprised, indicated Kirsteen, who happened to be in the room, with a wave of her hand, and withdrew a little in dignified watchfulness not without a shade of offence.

"Oh, Miss Douglas!" cried the elder lady, while the others fluttered round, enclosing Kirsteen in the circle. "We wish to have some things made, my daughters and I. And we were so anxious to see you. We know all your romantic story. And though, as the Duchess says, it may not be a very good example, yet we felt we must come at once and patronize you. It is so disinterested of you—and so romantic."

"So interesting—like a story out of a novel."

"So dramatic! It might go on the stage."

Kirsteen stood and listened with a surprised face and an angry heart while these exclamations fluttered round. Four ladies all rustling in silks and laces—no doubt likely to be excellent customers and therefore not to be too much discouraged, but each more exasperating than the other. Dramatic! On the stage! Kirsteen had been brought up to believe that the stage was a sort of vestibule of a region which the Scotch ministers of her period had no hesitation in naming. All the blood of the Douglases rushed to her cheeks.

"I think your ladyships must be deceived," she said; "we have no romantic stories nor stage plays here."

"Oh, you must not think you can escape, you interesting creature! For it was your friend Lady Charlotte, the great beauty, who told us all about it; and we all vowed that henceforward nobody should dress us but you."

"Lady Chatty is my friend indeed," said Kirsteen, "and she is a bonny creature; but what a friend may know is nothing to the world. And I am not the mistress here to undertake your work. Perhaps, Miss Jean, you will tell the ladies whether you can receive their orders or not. They are recommended, it would seem," she added, addressing her somewhat mortified and indignant principal over the heads of the new-comers, "by Lady Chatty, who is just full of fancies. And the work-room is very full. But you will know best yourself what you can do."

With this Kirsteen withdrew into the further part of the room, occupying herself again with the box of flowers which had already played its part in the beginning of her new life; and Miss Jean advanced into the middle of the scene. It had never before occurred to that good woman to treat a new customer, arriving in a coroneted carriage with liveries which lighted up the street, with indifference. But she was much mortified and affronted, and readily took up the cue.

"We are very busy, madam, as this young lady says. I cannot tell whether we can take the advantage of your ladyships' favours. We have gowns making for the Queen's Ball more than I remember for years. There is the Duchess herself, and Lady A., and Lady B., and the Marchioness, and Miss L., the Maid of Honour, and I cannot tell how many more—all old patronesses of mine," said Miss Jean with a slight courtesy that emphasized her pause.

"But oh, mamma, we can't be sent away! for I vowed to Lord John I would have a gown," cried one of the young ladies, "from" she glanced at Kirsteen with a little alarm, then added in a low voice with a little laugh, "*la belle couturière.*"

"My name is Brown, madam, and not Bell

—ye have perhaps made a mistake," said Miss Jean, grimly holding her ground.

This the young ladies received with much laughter and fluttering among themselves, as an excellent joke; while their mother, half indignant, half disappointed, eyed Miss Jean as if she would have liked to annihilate with a glance the presumptuous seamstress. But the refusal itself was such a new and startling effect, and the list of fashionable names was so overwhelming that any humiliation seemed better than failure. And Miss Jean after a while allowed herself to be mollified. Kirsteen on her part left the room, with a little offended pride mingled with some mischievous enjoyment. "They shall come to me with petitions not with orders," she said to herself, "before all's done."

Miss Jean kept a grave face for the rest of the day. She had ended by accepting with apparent reluctance and doubts as to the possibility of executing it, a large commission, and entering very readily into her new *rôle* had received the enthusiastic thanks of her new customers for her compliance with their request. Miss Jean had humour enough to be highly tickled by this turning of the tables, as well as practical good sense to see the enormous advantage to herself of assuming such a position should she be strong enough to do it. But at the same time it opened up grave questions which completely occupied her mind. Her business had grown into an important one through the best and simplest agency, by means of good work and punctuality and the other virtues that specially belong to honest trade, and rarely fail of success in the long run. She had that mingling of aristocratic predilections and democratic impulses which belongs to her race. An old family which was poor, a gentle lady of what she called real nobility, were always served with her best, and with a delicacy about payment for which nobody gave the old Scotswoman credit—but a haughty speech would fire her blood and change her aspect even from the most admired and genuine gentility —and a new peeress, much more a city lady, were subjects for lofty politeness and veiled disdain and princely bills. Kirsteen's suggestion had therefore fallen into prepared soil. The pride of Marg'ret's sister, though she had begun her life as a lady's maid, was scarcely less than that of Marg'ret's young mistress who had the blood of all the Douglases in her veins. And Miss Jean's keen practical faculty was sharpened by much experience and in her limited way by great knowledge of the world. She had now a problem before her of more importance than how best to make a skirt fall or a bodice fit, which had been till now the chief problems with which she had troubled herself.

She carried a grave countenance and many thoughts with her during the remainder of the day. Kirsteen, who noted this serious aspect with some alarm, made out to herself a little theory, to the effect that Miss Jean had taken serious offence and would not suffer the presence of an interloper who drew away the attention of her customers from herself—yet she did not fully adopt this either, in consideration of the great generosity towards her and unfailing kindness of Miss Jean. But the evening brought a certain suppressed excitement to both. It was a quiet house when all was over in the establishment,—the workrooms closed and dark, the workwomen all dispersed to their homes or asleep in their garrets,—in which the mistress of the household and her young guest were alone. They still occupied this relation to each other, Miss Jean treating Kirsteen with great ceremony as an honoured stranger, notwithstanding that her distinguished visitor was so condescending as to take part in the conduct of her work. When supper was over Miss Jean drew her chair towards the window which was open, for the spring by this time was advanced and nearly bursting into summer. The window admitted nothing more sweet than the faint and smoky lamplight of the streets into the room, to mingle with that of the candles; and though Chapel Street was always quiet, there were vague sounds from more distant streets, rolling of coaches and cries of the linkboys, which were scarcely musical. Nevertheless Miss Jean was able to say that the evening air coming in was sweet.

"And that reminds me, Miss Kirsteen," she said, "that ye have been quite a long time in London, three months and more. And how do you like what you have seen?"

"I like it very well," said Kirsteen. "It is not like the Hielands; there is no comparison to be made. But for a town it is a very good town—better than Glasgow, which is the only other town I ever saw."

"Glasgow!" said Miss Jean with disdain. "Glasgow has no more right to be named with London than the big lamp at Hyde Park Corner, which burns just tons of oil, with the little cruse in my kitchen. It's one of the points on which the Scots are just very foolish. They will bring forward Edinburgh, or that drookit hole of a Glasgow, as if they were fit to be compared with the real metropolis. In some ways the Scots, our country-folks, have more sense than all the rest of the world, but in others they're just ridiculous. I hope I've sense enough to see both sides, their virtues and their faults."

Kirsteen did not see how she was involved in this tirade, and consequently made no reply.

"But that's not what I was going to say, Miss Kirsteen. You have seen all about us now, both the house and the work and the place. And ye seem to have made up your mind that whatever is said to you, whether by the Duchess or the Duke or myself, ye will not be persuaded to go home."

Kirsteen, still very dubious as to the probable issue of these remarks, looked in Miss Jean's face with a smile and shook her head.

"Well, I will not say but what I think you very well able to manage your own affairs. Miss Kirsteen, that was a very clever thing ye did to-day."

"What was the clever thing?" asked Kirsteen surprised.

"Just to turn those leddies over in that

prideful way to me, as if they were not good enough to trouble our heads about. My word," cried Miss Jean with a laugh, "but ye made them dight their eyne, if ye will excuse a vulgar phrase. I'm thinking yon's the way to deal with newcomers," she said after a little pause.

"Well," said Kirsteen, "there is nobody so good as you, so far as I can hear, in all London. And it's a favour ye do them, to keep on and take all the trouble when ye have no need for it."

"I would not just say that—that I've no need—though I have put something by. And I would not say either that there was nobody so good. I've been good enough in my day, but I'm getting old—or at least older," said Miss Jean.

"We're all older to-day than we were yesterday," said Kirsteen cheerfully.

"Ay, but in my case it's more than that. I could never have struck out yon invention of yours for Lady Chatty with the silver gauze— though I saw it was just most beautiful when ye did it. And what's more, I could never have gotten the better of those leddies like you—I see it all, nobody clearer. Ye're just a gentlewoman ye see, Miss Kirsteen, and that's above a common person, whatever anybody may say."

"So far as I can see it makes very little difference," said Kirsteen, contradicting however the assurance in her own heart.

"It makes a great deal of difference; it gives a freedom in treating them that I cannot help feeling are my superiors. Well; this is just what I have to propose. Ye will not go home whatever anybody may say. And ye will not mairry, though I hear he's just a very nice gentleman. And ye will get cleverer and cleverer every day as ye get more knowledge of the world. It's just this, Miss Kirsteen; that you and me, we should enter into partnership and carry on the business together. And I think," said Miss Jean with modest confidence and a triumphant light in her eyes, "that between us we could just face the world."

"Into partnership!" cried Kirsteen in astonishment.

"Say nothing hastily, my dear—just go to your bed upon it. And we will not compromise an honoured name. We'll say Miss Brown and Miss Kirsteen—the English, who are very slow at the uptake, will think it's your family name, and that will compromise nobody," Miss Jean said.

CHAPTER XI.

It is difficult to calculate the exact moment at which it shall be found out by the members of a family that one of them has disappeared and gone away. It is easy to account for temporary absence: to think that the missing one has walked out too far, has been detained by some visit, has somehow been withdrawn unexpectedly and not by any will of his, from home. Kirsteen did not appear at breakfast; there were a few questions, "Where is Kirsteen?" "She will be with my mother." Her mother on the other hand was asking Jeanie who had taken up her breakfast, "Where is Kirsteen?" "She is gone out for a walk— or something," said Jeanie. It was not till after the second meal, at which there was no sign of her, that anything like alarm was excited. "Where is Kirsteen?" her father cried in what the children called his Bull of Bashan's voice. "I am not my sister's keeper —no doubt she's just away on one of her rovings," said Mary, whose mind however by this time was full of curiosity. She had been early struck by the complete disappearance of Kirsteen and every trace of her from about the place. Neither in the glen, nor by the linn, nor in the garden, was there any sign of her, no evidence that she had passed by either in parlour or in kitchen. She had not been in her mother's room. Mrs. Douglas had already asked for more than a dozen times where was Kirsteen?—requiring her for a hundred things. It was only however when she found Marg'ret anxiously attempting to do Kirsteen's special business, to pick up the lost stitches in Mrs. Douglas's knitting, to arrange her pillows and help her to move that a real suspicion darted through Mary's mind. Could Kirsteen have gone away? and could Marg'ret know of it? On being interrogated the boys and Jeanie declared that neither on the way to school nor at the merchant's which they had passed on their return home, had any trace of her been seen. And Mary thought that Marg'ret's eyes were heavy, that she looked like a person who had been up all night, or who had been crying a great deal, and observed, which was more extraordinary still, that she alone showed no curiosity about Kirsteen. Had all been natural it was she who would have been most easily alarmed. This acute observation helped Mary to the full truth, or at least to as much of it as it was possible to find out. "Where's Kirsteen?" she said suddenly in Marg'ret's ear, coming down upon her unawares, after she had left Mrs. Douglas's room.

Marg'ret was drying her eyes with her apron, and the sound of a sob, which she had not time to restrain, breathed into the air as Mary came upon her. "Oh, what a start ye gave me!" she answered as soon as she could recover her voice.

"Where is Kirsteen?" said Mary again. "You cannot conceal it from me,—where is she, and what have ye done with her? I will not tell upon you if you will explain it to me."

"Kirsteen—what is all this stir about Kirsteen? She will just have gane up the hill or down the linn, or maybe she'll have gone to see her old auntie at the toun." Here Marg'ret betrayed herself by a heave of her solid shoulders that showed she was weeping, though she attempted with a broken laugh to conceal the fact. "It's no so many—diversions —the poor thing has."

"You know where she is, Marg'ret—and ye've helped her to get away."

"Me!" cried Marg'ret, with convulsive indignation; then she made a great effort to recover herself. "How should I ken where she is? Yes, I do that! She's on her way home no doubt over the hillside—or down the loch coming back."

"You'll perhaps tell me then what you're greetin' for?"

"I have plenty of things to make me greet," Marg'ret said; then after a pause—"Who said I was greetin'? I just canna be fashed with endless questions, and the haill family rantin' and ravin'. Ye can go and find your sister for yourself."

"And so I will—or at least I'll satisfy myself," said Mary with a determination which, though mild and quiet, was not less assured than the bold resolutions of Kirsteen. She went softly up stairs and proceeded to visit her sister's room, where her keen perceptions soon showed her a certain amount of disarray. "She cannot have two gowns on her back, both the blue and the brown," said Mary to herself. "She would never put on her spencer and bonnet to go out on the hillside. She would not have taken that little box with her that she keeps her treasures in and that aye stands by her bedside, had she only gone to see Auntie Eelen. She's just gone away—and there is an end of it." Mary stood reflecting for some time after she came to this decision.

It did not distress her for the moment, but lit a spark of invention, a keener light than usual in her mild brown eyes that never had been full of light like Kirsteen's. After a few minutes of consideration, she went to her own room and dressed herself carefully to go out—carefully but not too well, not with the spencer, the Sunday garment, which Kirsteen had taken. Mary put on an old cloth pelisse, and a brown bonnet which was not her best. "I am not going on a journey, I will only be about the doors," she said to herself.

Marg'ret was standing outside when she came down stairs, with a look of anxiety on her face, which changed into subdued derision when Mary appeared. "Ye'll be going after her?" she said. "Well, I wish ye may find her; but if she's gane, as ye think, she'll have gotten a long start."

"I'm going—to put some things right," said Mary enigmatically. The consciousness that Marg'ret stood and watched as she went along the road quickened her senses, and confirmed her in her conviction. It was afternoon, and the wintry sun was shining red through a haze of frost out of the western sky. It dazzled her with its long level lines of light as she walked down the road. There would be a moon that night, so that the visitor who was expected at Drumcarro would have light enough to ride home by, however late he might be; yet he was a little late, and Mary was anxious to meet him at some distance from the house. She walked very quickly for about half a mile towards the hamlet, in which the merchant's shop stood surrounded by three or four cottages. And then she perceived in the distance riding over the little bridge which crossed the stream, the red light catching the metal buttons of his riding-coat and the silver top of his whip, the trim figure of Glendochart coming towards her. At such a distance his grey hair and the lines of his face were of course quite invisible, and he rode like a young man, with all the advantages of good horsemanship and a fine horse to set off his well-formed figure. Mary slackened her pace at once. She looked at him with a little sigh. What a happy windfall would that be to one, which to another was a hardship and misfortune! She herself would not have objected at all to Glendochart's age. She would have liked him the better for it, as likely to make a more complaisant husband. However, it was not to her that he had come wooing, but to Kirsteen, with whom he had no chance, so troublesome and contrary were the decisions of fate.

Mary gave a sigh to this thought, and turned over in her mind rapidly the purpose with which she had come out and what she was to say. She decided that even if Kirsteen came back, which was not probable, she could do no harm by warning Glendochart. It would save him a refusal at least, it would let him know the real state of affairs. She walked more and more slowly as the horseman advanced. There was a corner of the road where a projecting rock formed a sort of angle, shutting out a little the noise of the brawling burn and making a natural halting-place. She contrived that she should meet the wayfarer here. Glendochart perceived her as he came along before they actually met. She appeared just beyond the corner, recognized him, paused a little, and then waving her hand to him turned back. Nothing could be more evident than that she had something to say. When he had reached the corner he found her standing, modest and quiet, within the shadow of the rock.

"I hope nothing's wrong, Miss Mary, at the house?" he said hurriedly.

"Well," she said, "that is as may be. I have perhaps done a bold thing, but I was wanting a word with ye, Glendochart, before you go on."

"What is the matter?" he cried with alarm. He was evidently very unwilling to be detained. "Your father is expecting me,

Miss Mary," he said, "and I hope your sister——"

"It is just about Kirsteen, Glendochart, that I wish to speak to you."

"What is it?" he said. "Is she ill?—has anything happened?"

"There has just this happened," said Mary. "I would not let ye have a trouble or a shock that I could spare you—Kirsteen has left her home."

"Left her home!" His ruddy colour disappeared in a moment; he threw himself off his horse. "What do you mean? I do not understand you!" he cried.

"Glendochart," said Mary seriously, "nobody has told me; but I don't think you were meaning to make any secret of it, that it was after Kirsteen you were coming to our house."

The elderly lover coloured a little. "I would not hide it from you that that was my intention. It was her," he said with a little apologetic wave of his hand, "that I saw first of the family, and upon her I fixed my fancy; not that all the daughters of Drumcarro were not worthy of every admiration."

"Oh, Glendochart, ye need not apologize. Fancy is free, as is well known. I saw it well from the first, for a sister's eyne are quick to observe; but, if ye will believe me, the one that never noticed was just Kirsteen herself."

"Not possible!" said the wooer, with this time a little flush of offence.

"But it is just very possible—her mind was not set on anything of the kind. And it was her opinion that just friendship and kindness—for all the family——"

"Did she bid ye tell me this?"

"No, no—she said nothing, poor thing. If she had but spoken either to me, that could have explained for her, or to you that would never have forced her——"

"Forced her!" cried the old beau, who had always prided himself upon the fact that his was neither the form nor the eye.

"Which youthful maidens wont to fly."

"Well, I know that!" said Mary with fervour; "and there are few that would have needed any fleeching, if I may say so. But I reckon that she just heard it from my father, very suddenly. My father is a dour man, Glendochart. Whatever ye may have to say he will never hear ye speak. He will listen to the boys—whiles—but to us never. Just you must do this, or you must do that, and not a word more."

"Drumcarro," said Glendochart, now full of passion, "has done me a cruel wrong in putting my suit before any lady in such a way. Your sister was free to have taken it or left it, Miss Mary. Me press a proposition that was not acceptable!—not for all the world!"

"I am well aware of that," said Mary with feeling; "but my father is a dour man, and he would say, 'Not a word! just take the offer and be thankful.' And indeed," said Mary diffidently, "in most cases there would be little difficulty, but Kirsteen is one that is very much set upon her own way."

"She had but to say so," cried the offended suitor; "I promise she would have had no more trouble with me!"

"Oh, Glendochart, do not be angry— I am just sure that he would not let her say a word. She has not been like herself this week past. It has just been on her mind night and day. And at last she has taken a despair, seeing no way of getting out of it—and she has gone away."

"I am not in the habit," said Glendochart, "of finding myself a bugbear. I would seem to cut a pretty figure in all this—a sort of old Robin Gray," he said with a furious laugh. "I am sure I am obliged to you all! 'With tears in his e'e, said Jenny, for their sake will ye marry me?' I beg to say, Miss Mary, that this was not my attitude at all."

"Do you need to say that to me, Glendochart?" said Mary reproachfully. "Oh, no! nor even to poor Kirsteen either, who would have been fain to hear every word ye had to say—for she was very fond of ye, Glendochart."

"It is a strange way of showing it," he said, but he was mollified in spite of himself.

"As we all were. It will be a great heart-break and a great downfall if ye come no more to the house because of Kirsteen. But she would have been fain, fain to hear whatever ye had to say, if it had not been——"

"What hindered her, then?" he said.

"It's no for me to betray her secrets," said Mary, "and indeed she never told them to me, for she was not one that opened her heart. But there is little that can be hidden from a sister's eye. And it was just this—there was one before ye, Glendochart. If she had seen you first I am very sure she would never have thought of him—for to my mind there's no more comparison—but, poor thing, she had given her word. Take what you offered her and be mansworn to the other lad was all that was before her; and no true to you either, for she would never have dared to tell you."

Glendochart was still much offended and disturbed. He had fastened his horse to a tree, and was now pacing about the road within the corner of the rock with mingled rage and pain. But he was moved by the soft voice and pleading accents of the very mild and pleasing intercessor, whose suggestion of her own superior taste was put in with so much gentle insistence. Mary's eyes, which were cast down when he looked at her, but raised with much meaning to his face when he did not seem to be observing, softened his mood in spite of himself.

"If that was the case," he said, "there was perhaps an excuse for her, though when she knew it was so she should not have encouraged and drawn on—another man."

It was Mary's policy to give a very charitable representation of Kirsteen's action, and it was also quite congenial to her feelings, for she was not spiteful nor malicious, notwithstanding that it seemed to be a very sensible thing to turn her sister's failure to her own advantage if that could be done.

"Glendochart," she said, "there's some things in which gentlemen never can understand the heart of a girl. She had no thought of encouraging and drawing on. That never came into her head. She liked you well, and she thought no harm in showing it."

"Because," cried Glendochart, with mingled offence and emotion, "she thought I was an old man, and out of the question. That is easy to see—"

"It was not that," said Mary softly. "She saw that you were kind to all of us—every one. Perhaps she may have thought that you had—other intentions. And oh," said the gentle girl, raising her eyes to his, "it made such a difference to us all! It's been so lightsome and so heartsome, Glendochart, to see ye always coming. There is little diversion at Drumcarro. My father is a very dour man, wrapped up in the boys, and my mother, she is always ailing, poor body; and we see nobody; and to have you coming just like sunshine, with a smile to one and a kind word to another, and thinking no shame to be pleasant even to me— that ye thought nothing of—or little Jeanie, that is but a bairn."

Glendochart was very much touched. He took Mary's hand in both his. " Do not say that I thought nothing of you, for that would be far from the case ; and how am I to thank you now for taking so much thought for me ? You have just behaved like an angel so far as I can see, both to me and to her."

"Oh, Glendochart, not that! But just what I could do in the way of kindness," she said.

CHAPTER XII.

THE result of this interview was that Glendochart turned and rode home, very full of wrath and disappointment, yet soothed in his *amour propre* by the kind expedient of the angelic girl, who returned to Drumcarro very demurely with the consciousness that her time and exertions had not been lost. She had indeed decided perhaps too summarily that Kirsteen's disappearance was a permanent one; but as the day crept on, and there was no appearance of her return, the temporary qualm which had come over Mary's mind dispersed again. She had the satisfaction of seeing that her father was very much disturbed by the non-appearance of Glendochart. He came out of his den from time to time, and took a turn round the house and stood out at the gate straining his eyes along the road. "Is it Kirsteen ye are looking for, father?" Mary said. Drumcarro asked with a fierce exclamation what he was caring about Kirsteen. Let her go to the devil if she liked. What he was looking for was quite a different person. "But maybe," said Mary, "the other person will not be coming if Kirsteen is not here." Her father asked fiercely, what she knew about it? But he was evidently impressed by the remark, for he went up and down stairs and out to the side of the linn, shouting for Kirsteen in a way that filled all the echoes. "Where is Kirsteen all this day, and why cannot she come when her father is crying on her? He will just bring down the house," Mrs. Douglas had said, putting her hands upon her ears. "She might maybe have a headache, and be lying down upon her bed," said little Jeanie, to whom a similar experience had once occurred, and who had felt the importance it gave her.

The anxieties of the family were soothed by this and other suggestions until the early wintry night fell and it was discovered that nobody had seen her, or knew anything about her. Marg'ret in her kitchen had been in an intense suppressed state of excitement all day, but it had not been discovered by any one save the astute Mary that she showed no curiosity about Kirsteen, and asked no questions. When it came to be bedtime the whole household was disturbed. The boys had gone out over the hill, and towards the merchant's along the road to see if any trace could be found of her, while Jeanie stood under the birch-trees—now denuded of all their yellow leaves—outside, looking out through the dark with all that sense of desolation and mystery which is in the idea of night to the mind of a child. Jeanie stood very quiet, crying to herself, but thinking she heard footsteps and all kinds of mysterious movements about her, and fully making up her mind to see Kirsteen carried home, murdered or dead of cold and exposure, or something else that was equally terrible and hopeless; and though she would have been overjoyed, yet she would also have been a little disappointed had she seen Kirsteen walk in with no harm or injury, which was also more or less the frame of mind of Jock and Jamie, who fully expected to stumble over their sister among the withered bracken, or to see her lying by the side of the road.

There was however a moment of mute despair when they all came back and looked at each other for an explanation of the mystery. Then the children burst out crying one after the other, the boys resisting the impulse till nature was too strong for them, and producing a louder and more abrupt explosion from the fact of the attempted restraint. Their father stood looking round upon them all, his fierce eyes blazing, looking for some way of venting the rage that was in him. The lass disappeared, confound her! And Glendochart drawing back, the devil flee away with him! Drumcarro was indeed in evil case. When Jock, who was the last to give way, burst out without a moment's notice into a violent boo-hoo, his father caught him suddenly a box on the ear which sent him spinning across the room. "Haud your confounded tongue, can't ye —and no wake your mother." "Eh, my poor laddie! Ye need not punish him for me, for here I am, and what is the matter with everybody?" said the weak voice of Mrs. Douglas at the door. She had been left alone during all this excitement, and her repeated calls had brought nobody. So that querulous, displeased, and full of complaining, unable to bear the silence and the want of information, the poor soul had wrapped herself in the first garments she could find, and tottered down stairs. She appeared a curious mass of red flannel, chintz, and tartan, one wrapped over the other. "What is the matter?" she said, looking eagerly round upon the troubled family. "Oh, mother," cried little Jeanie weeping, running to her and hiding her face and her tears in one of these confused wrappings. "Kirsteen has gone away. She's *run* away," said Jeanie, afraid not to be believed—and then the commotion was increased by a wail from the mother, who sank in a state of collapse into her large chair, and by the rush of Marg'ret from the kitchen, who perceiving what had happened flew to give the necessary help. "Could you not all hold your tongues, and let her get her night's rest in peace?" Marg'ret cried. The scene was dismal enough, and yet had thus a rude comedy mingled with its real pain. Drumcarro stalked away when this climax of confusion was reached. "I was a fool ever to mind one of them," he said. "Ye little whinging deevil, get out o' my way. You're no better than a lassie yourself."

Mary had done her best to save the story from becoming public by warning the expectant suitor, who on his side had thought himself safely out of the ridicule of it by his quick withdrawal. But the voices of the servants and the children were not to be silenced. "Have ye heard the news?" said Duncan the carter at the toll-bar. "The maister up at the house is neither to haud nor to bind. Our Kirsteen has ta'en her fit in her hand and run away, the Lord kens where, for fear he would mairry her against her will to auld Glendochart." "Eh, do ye ken what's happened?" said Marg'ret's help in the kitchen as soon as she could find an excuse to run to the merchant's. "Miss Kirsteen, she's aff to the ends of the earth, and the mistress near deed with trouble, and Marg'ret raging just like a sauvage beast." The boys whispered it to their mates at school with a certain sense of distinction, as of people to whom something out of the common had happened, and Jeanie who had no one else to communicate the wonderful fact to, told the little girl that brought the letters, by whom it was published far and near. Miss Eelen heard it the next morning by means of Jock, who rode the pony over almost before daylight to inquire if his sister had been seen there.

"Indeed she might have been too proud to have had the offer of Glendochart," the old lady said. "He should just take Mary instead." "He will maybe think that's not the same thing," said Mr. Pyper, the minister, who went over to the town in his gig soon after about some Presbytery business, and to hear what people were saying. "Well it will be very near the same thing," Miss Eelen said.

This was how it had come to the ears of the Duke and Duchess and all the best society in the county, who were immensely entertained, and told a hundred stories about the gallant wooer whose attempt at courtship had been so disastrous. He went away himself the next day, sending a letter to Drumcarro to say that he had heard that his suit was disagreeable to the young lady, and that nothing could induce him to press it after he knew this fact; but that he hoped on his return to pay his respects to Mrs. Douglas and the young ladies. Drumcarro was not to be spoken to by any member of his family after this happened for several days. Had he met with the gallant old gentleman who had thus, in his own opinion, retired so gracefully, it is to be feared the trim Glendochart might have found his martial science of but little avail against "the auld slave-driver's" brutal energy and strength. But after a while Mr. Douglas calmed down. He flung Kirsteen's little possessions out of doors, and swore with many oaths that whoever named that hizzy's name again should leave his house on the moment. But when Glendochart, coming back in the spring, came out formally to pay a visit at Drumcarro, bringing boxes of French chocolate and other tokens of his residence abroad, the laird, though he gave him the briefest salutation, did not knock him down, which was what the family feared. And by dint of a diplomacy which would have done credit to any ambassador, Mary continued so to close her mother's mouth that no reference should be made to the past. Mrs. Douglas was too much afraid of her husband to introduce Kirsteen's name, but she was ready with a hundred little allusions. "Ah, Glendochart, when ye were here last! That was before our last misfortune. I will never be so well again as I was in those days, when I had one by me that never forgot her mother." She would have sympathized with him and claimed his sympathy in this furtive way from the moment of his arrival. But Mary had taken by this time very much the upper hand and brought her mother into great subjection. "Ye will just drive him away if ye say a word." "I am sure," Mrs. Douglas said weeping, "her name never crosses my lips." "But what does that matter when you are just full of allusions and talk of her that's away." "Alas! there is another that I might be meaning," said the poor mother; "two of them, bonny lassies as ever lived, and one with weans of her own that I will never see." "Oh, mother, why should ye make such a work about them that never think of you? They would have bided at home if their hearts had been here. But it's a grand thing for the boys and Jeanie," said the astute elder sister, "that Glendochart should come back. It sets us right with the world, and see the things he's always bringing them." "Mainy sweeties are not good for children, though thae chocolate ones are maybe wholesome enough," said Mrs. Douglas. "And what does he ever do for them but bring them sweeties?" "Mother, it's just education for them to hear such a man speak," cried Mary, which silenced Mrs. Douglas at the end.

Mary apparently felt the full force of what she said. She listened to him devoutly; she persuaded him to talk with little murmurs of pleasure. "Eh, it's just as good as a book to hear ye, Glendochart"—and other such ascriptions of praise. Few men are quite superior to this kind of flattery, and one who has been slighted in another quarter and has felt the absence of any just appreciation of his deserts, is more than usually open to it. Glendochart fell into his old habit of frequent visits to Drumcarro, and he was pleased by the universal interest in him—the delight of the young ones, and the gentle devotion of Mary. A soft regret, a tender respect was in her tone. The only time in which she ever displayed a consciousness of the past was when she thanked him with almost tears in her eyes for coming: "Which we could never have expected." It was not, however, until a day in spring, in the month of April, when the beauty of the country was awakening, that the old gentleman was completely subjugated. The linn was subdued from the volume of its wintry torrent, but was roaring over the rocks still with the fulness of spring showers one bright afternoon when he met Mary on the road taking a walk, as she said. They returned, without any intention passing the house and continuing their walk unconsciously, drawn on by the tumult of the stream. Glendochart stood at the head of the little glen, and looked down the ravine with many thoughts. Mary had drawn aside from its edge. "I cannot go down that dreadful way. It makes me giddy," said Mary. "I never liked that steep bank; the others run up and down just like goats—but not me! If ye will excuse my weakness, Glendochart, and go a little round by the road, we'll come out at the foot just the same."

Now it had been with a rush of recollection that Glendochart had come to the linn side. He remembered well how Kirsteen had rushed on before him as airy as a feather, trying the stones with her light weight, to find which was most steady, like a bird alighting upon them, putting out her hand to help him—she the young lady who ought to have been indebted to him for help. And he remembered the slip he had made and his fall, and the tremble in her voice which he had feared meant laughter, and the effort he had made to look as if a tumble on the wet sod was nothing, a thing he did not mind. Mary had far more sense to go round by the road. He felt himself in so much better a position agreeing with her that it was too steep for a lady, and gallantly guiding her round the safer way. It was a soft evening with no wind, and a delightful spring sky full of brightness and hope. In the spring a young man's fancy lightly turns to thoughts of love, and the fancy of an old young gentleman who has been led to think of these matters and then has been cruelly disappointed, is if anything more easily awakened. Glendochart gave Mary his arm to help her along the gentler round of the road, and his mouth was opened and he spoke.

"Miss Mary," he said, "ye were very kind a few months back in a matter which we need not now enter into. I can never cease to be grateful to you for the warning ye gave me. And ye have been more than kind since I came home. It has been a great pleasure to come to Drumcarro, though I did it at first mostly out of a sense of duty. But to see you gave it a charm."

"Oh, Glendochart, you are very kind to say so," said Mary. "We just all of us have a debt to you that we can never repay."

"Not a word about debt, or I would soon

be on the wrong side of the balance. It has been a great part of the pleasure of my life to come—but now I will have to be thinking whether I should come again."

"Oh, Glendochart! and wherefore so?" cried Mary with alarm in her eyes.

"My dear young lady," said the Highland gentleman, "I am getting an old man—I was mangrown (and perhaps a trifle more) before ye were born."

She had said "Oh, no!" softly while he was speaking, with a gentle pressure upon his arm—and now when he paused she lifted her dove's eyes and said, "What does that matter?" in tones as soft as the wood-pigeon's coo.

"You must understand me," he said, "which I am afraid was more than your sister, poor thing, ever did—I have been experiencing a great change of feeling. She was a bright young creature full of pretty ways—and I was just beguiled—the like of that may blind a man for a time, but when his eyes are opened to the knowledge of a more excellent way—that he had not observed before—"

"It is true," said Mary in a faltering voice; "my poor Kirsteen had a great deal of the child in her. And it would not be my part to be affronted if ye had seen another that was maybe better adapted to make you happy. Oh, no! it would be ill my part—though I might regret."

"Ye have no guess," said Glendochart with a tender touch of the hand that clung to his arm, "who that other is, who is the only person I will ever think of?"

"No," said Mary with a sigh. "I'm not sure that I want to hear—but that's a poor sentiment and it shall not be encouraged by me. On the contrary it will not be my fault if that lady—who will have a happy lot, I am sure—does not find kind friends here."

"If she does not it will be most unnatural," said Glendochart, "for the person I am meaning is just yourself and no other. And if ye think she will have a happy lot—my dear, take it—for it will never be offered to any woman but you."

"Oh, Glendochart!" said Mary casting down her eyes.

It was very different from his wooing of Kirsteen and in many ways much more satisfactory—for far from running away in horror of his suit, which is a thing to pique the pride of any man, Mary was unfeignedly proud of having won the prize which she had at once felt, failing Kirsteen, it would be a good thing to keep in the family. She saved her old lover every trouble. She would not have him go to her father, which was what he proposed with great spirit to do at once. "No," she said, "it is me that must tell him. My father is a strange man; he is little used to the like of you; but I know all his ways. And I will tell him; for ye must mind, Glendochart, if ye mairry me that I will not have ye taigled with all my family. The boys and little Jeanie now and then if ye please for a short visit, or my mother for a change of air, but just at your pleasure, and not like a thing you're obliged to do. I will take that into my own hand. Ye can leave it all to me."

Glendochart rode away that night with great satisfaction in his mind. He felt that he had wiped out his reproach; after having failed to marry Kirsteen it was a necessity to vindicate himself by marrying somebody— and he particularly felt (after the consolation that had been drawn from Mary's gentle speeches and ways) that to marry out of this very house where he had been slighted would be the most complete vindication. And he was delighted with his second choice; her good taste, her good sense, her clear perception of all that was necessary, filled him with satisfaction and content. He rode away with something of the ardour of a young man joined to the more reasonable satisfaction of an old one, in the consciousness of having secured the most devoted of housekeepers, a lady who would "look well at his tablehead," who would take care of his interests and would not even allow him to be taigled with her family. He kissed his hand to his bonny Mary, and his soul was filled with delightful anticipations. There was no doubt she was a bonny creature, far more correct and satisfactory than that gilpie Kirsteen with her red hair. Glendochart was thus guilty of the vulgar unfaithfulness of disparaging his own ideal—but it is a sin less heinous in an old lover than in a young one—for how many ideals must not the old gentleman have lived through?

Mary walked in straight to her father's door—who took as little notice of Glendochart as possible in these days. He was sitting with a map of the old Douglas property before him, painfully ruminating whether he could anyhow squeeze out of the family living enough to buy a corner of land that was in the market; and wondering, with a sort of forlorn fury, whether Sandy or even Sandy's son, might be able to gather all that land back again to the Douglas name. This was his ideal; all others, such as love, or affection, or the ties of human fellowship having died out of his mind long ago, if they had ever occupied any place there. He looked up angrily as Mary came in. What could she want, the useless woman-creature that was good for nothing, never could bring a penny into the house, but only take out of it as long as she should live?

"Well! what are you wanting now?" he said sharply.

"I am wanting to speak to you," Mary said.

"A fool would understand that, since ye've come here; which is a place where there's no room for weemen. Speak out what you've got to say, and leave me quiet, which is all I desire from ye."

"I am afraid," said Mary sweetly, "that I will have to give ye a little trouble, father; though it will save you a good deal of fash later."

"Give me trouble is what you do night and day. Save me fash is what I've never known."

"It will be so now," said Mary, "for to provide for your daughters would be a great fash to you, and one that would go sore against the grain. So you should be glad, father, however little ye think of us, when we can provide for ourselves."

"How are ye going to do that?" said Drumcarro derisively. "No man will have ye. I'm sick of the very name of ye," he said; "I wish there was not a woman in the house."

"Well," said Mary, with imperturbable good temper, "ye will soon be quit of one. For I'm going to be marriet, and I've come to tell you."

"To be marriet! I don't believe it; there's no man will look at ye," said the indignant father.

"It is true we never see any men," said Mary; "but one is enough, when ye can make up your mind to him. Father, we would like to name an early day, seeing that he has been disappointed already, and that there is no time to lose. It is Glendochart I am intending to marry," she said demurely, looking him in the face.

"Glendochart!" he got up from his chair and swore a large round oath. "That hizzy's leavings!" he said. "Have ye no pride?"

"I will have a great deal of pride when I'm settled in my own house," replied Mary. "He will be here to-morrow to settle everything; but I thought I would just tell you to-night. And I hope, father," she added with great gravity, "that seeing I'm here to protect him you will keep a civil tongue in your head."

CHAPTER XIII.

These events were communicated by letter to the members of the firm of Misses Brown and Kirsteen, Dressmakers to her Majesty, Chapel Street, Mayfair. The medium of communication was Marg'ret, whose letters to her sister had become, to the vast enlightenment of the only member of the Drumcarro household who was qualified to collect circumstantial evidence, suspiciously frequent. Mary, it may be supposed, had not much time to give to correspondence, while the facts lately recorded were going on; but when all was settled she slipped into Marg'ret's hand a letter containing the important news. " I am not asking where she is—I am thinking that through your sister, Miss Jean, in London, ye might possibly find a means of getting it to Kirsteen's hand."

"It's an awfu' expense for postage, and a double letter. I will just be ruined," said Marg'ret; "and my sister Jean might not ken anything about the address."

"You could always try," said Mary derisively.

"That's true, I might try—for she's a very knowledgeable person, my sister Jean; but that will make a double letter—and how is the like of me to get a frank or any easement?"

"I will ask Glendochart—for he has plenty of friends in the Parliament houses."

"I will have none from Glendochart! The Lord be praised, I have still a shilling in my pouch to ware upon my friends."

"Ye are just a jealous woman for your friends," said Mary with a laugh of triumph.

"Maybe I am that and maybe I am not. I would neither wile away my sister's jo nor tak what anither's left," cried Marg'ret with unreasonable indignation. But Mary turned away with a demure smile. She had no such ridiculous prejudices. And perhaps it will be best to give in full her letter to Kirsteen explaining how everything came about.

"DEAR CHRISTINA,—I am writing you a letter on the risk of perhaps not finding you; but I have the less fear of that that I have always been conscious Marg'ret Brown knew very well at the time where you were to be found. And the letters she gets and sends away have just been ridiculous. I would say one in a fortnight, never less. It stands to reason that it would not be her sister Jean she was writing to so often. So I made sure you were for something in it. And therefore it is with no little confidence that I send this. If ye do not receive it, you will not be able to blame me, for I will have done everything I could.

"And I have a great deal to tell you, and in particular about Mr. Henry Campbell of Glendochart, who was abroad for his health in the beginning of the year, and afterwards took up his old practice of visiting at Drumcarro, which was, you know, very well liked by every person: for he was very kind to the children, and brought them beautiful boxes of fine sweeties made of chocolate from Paris, which they consumed from morning till night, my mother being always afraid it would put their stomachs out of order; but no harm followed. Now you know, Christina, that in former times when you were at home it was commonly believed by all the family that Glendochart was coming for you. But it would appear that this had been a mistake. Perhaps it was that his fancy was not fixed then between us two, being sisters and about the same age, which I am told is a thing that sometimes happens. But anyhow the other day him and me being on the road down to the linn—not that awful steep road that you were always trying to break your own neck and other folks' upon, but the road round that goes by the side of the hill—he began to talk to me very seriously, and to say that he had long been thinking upon a Person that would make him a good wife. And I said—that he might see there was no ill-will or disappointment—that I was sure she would be a happy woman, and that she should always find friends at Drumcarro. And on this he took courage and told me he hoped so, for it was just Me that was the Person, and that the offer he made me was one that he would not make to any other woman. I was very much surprised, thinking always that it had been You—but you being gone, and there being no possibility in that quarter, and being always very favourable to Glendochart myself and sure he would make a very good man—besides that it would be real good for my mother to get a change of air from time to time, and that it is better to be a married woman in your own good house, than a lass at home with nothing but what her father will lay out upon her (and you know how little that is), or even an Old Maid like Auntie Eelen, though in many ways she is very comfortable. But taking all things into consideration I just thought I would take Glendochart, who is a very creditable person in every way, and a fine figure of a man; though not so very young. And I hope you will have no feeling upon the subject as if I did wrong to take what they call my sister's leavings, and other coarse things of that kind. For of course if you had wanted him you would have taken him when you had the offer, and it can do you no harm that another should have him, when you would not have him yourself.

"So after all, dear Christina, this is just to tell you that on the 1st of June we are to be married by Mr. Pyper at Drumcarro. I will wear a habit which it was my desire should be of green cloth, with a little gold lace; but they all rose against me, saying that there was an old rhyme to the effect that—

> 'The bride that is married in green
> Her sorrow will soon be seen'—

so I yielded about that, and it is to be French grey, with a little silver upon the coat-tails and the cuffs and pockets, and a grey hat with a silver band and a grey veil; which will be very pretty and useful too, for grey does not show the dust as red would have done, which was what my mother wanted, being the fashion in her time. We will stay quietly for a week or two at our own house of Glendochart, and then he has promised that he will take me to London. I hope you will let me know by Marg'ret where I can find you, and I will come and see you. Perhaps in the changed circumstances you would rather not see Henry, though he has a most kindly feeling, and would never think of being guided by my father's ban, which you might be sure would be placed upon you. Neither would I ever give in to it, especially as a married woman, owing no duty but to her husband, and him a real enlightened man. So there would be no difference made either by me or him, but very glad to see you, either in the place where you are, or at Glendochart, or wherever we might be. If I don't hear anything more particular I will come to Miss Jean Brown's when I get to London in hopes that she will tell me where to find you, especially as I cannot be in London without taking the opportunity to get a new gown or perhaps two, and I hear she is very much patronized by the first people, and in a very good position as a mantua-maker.

"Now, dear Christina, I hope you will send me a word by Marg'ret about your address; but anyway I will come to Miss Brown's and find you out, and in the meantime I am very glad to have had the opportunity of letting you know all our news, and I remain

"Your affectionate sister,

"MARY DOUGLAS.

"P.S. My mother keeps just in her ordinary."

This letter was given to Kirsteen out of the cover which Miss Jean opened with great precaution on account of the writing that was always to be found on the very edge of the paper where the letter was folded, and under the seal. Miss Jean shook her head while she did so and said aloud that Marg'ret was very wasteful, and what was the good of so many letters. "For after all," she said, "news will keep; and so long as we know that we are both well what is the object in writing so often? I got a letter, it's not yet three weeks ago, and here's another. But one thing is clear, it's not for me she writes them, and we must just try to get her a few franks and save her siller." But she gave what she called a *skreigh* as soon as she had read half a page. "It's your sister that's going to be married?" that was indeed a piece of news that warranted the sending of a letter. Kirsteen read hers with a bright colour and sparkling eyes. She was angry, which was highly unreasonable, though I have remarked it in women before. She felt it to be an offence that Glendochart had been able to console himself so soon. And she was specially exasperated to think that it was upon Mary his choice had fallen. Mary! to like her as well as me! Kirsteen breathed to herself, feeling, perhaps, that her intimate knowledge of her sister's character did not increase her respect for Mary. "Having known me to decline on a range of lower feelings." These words were not written then, nor probably had they been written, would they have reached Kirsteen, but she fully entered into the spirit of them. "Mary! when it was me he wanted!" She did not like the idea at all.

"Yes," she said sedately, "so it appears;" but her breathing was a little quickened, and there was no pleasure in her tone.

"And is your sister so like you?" said Miss Jean.

"She is not like me at all," said Kirsteen. "She is brown-haired and has little colour, and very smooth and soft in all her ways." Kirsteen drew a long breath and the words that she had spoken reminded her of other words. She thought to herself, but did not say it, "Now Jacob was a smooth man." And then poor Kirsteen flamed with a violent blush and said to herself, "What a bad girl I am! Mary has never been false or unkind to me—and why should not she take Glendochart when I would not take him? And why should the poor man never have anybody to care for him because once he cared for the like of me?"

Miss Jean did not, of course, hear this, but she saw that something was passing in Kirsteen's mind that was more than she chose to say. And, like a kind woman, she went on talking in order that the balance might come right in the mind of her young companion. "They will be coming to London," she said, "just when the town is very *throng*—and that is real confusing to folk from the country. If it will be pleasing to you, Miss Kirsteen, I will ask them to their dinner; that is, if they will not think it a great presumption in the like of me."

To tell the truth Kirsteen herself felt that Marg'ret's sister was not exactly the person to entertain Glendochart and Mary, who were both of the best blood in the country; but she was too courteous to say this. "It would be very kind of you, Miss Jean," she said, "but I am not sure that it would be pleasing to me. Perhaps it would be better to let them just take their own gait and never to mind."

"I have remarked," said Miss Jean, "in

my long experience that a quiet gentleman from the country when he comes up to London with his new married wife, has often very few ideas about where he is to take her to. He thinks that he will be asked to his dinner by the chief of his name, and that auld friends will just make it a point to be very ceevil. And so they would perhaps at a quiet time; but when the town is so *throng*, and people's minds fixed on what will be the next news of the war, and everybody taken up with themselves, it is not so easy to mind upon country friends. And I have seen them that come to London with very high notions just extremely well pleased to come for an evening to a countrywoman, even when she was only a mantua-maker. But it shall be just whatever way you like, and you know what my company is and who I would ask."

"Oh, it is not for that!" cried Kirsteen. By this time she knew very well what Miss Jean's company was. There was an old Mrs. Gordon, who had very high connections and "called cousins" with a great many fine people, and had a son with Lord Wellington's army, but who was very poor and very glad to be received as an honoured guest in Miss Jean's comfortable house. And there was the minister of the Scots church in the city, who announced to everybody on all occasions that there was nobody he had a higher respect for than Miss Jean, and that her name was well known in connection with all the Caledonian charities in London. And there was Miss Jean's silk-mercer, to whom she gave her large and valuable custom, and who was in consequence Miss Jean's very humble servant, and always happy to carve the turkey or help the beef at her table, and act as "landlord" to her guests—which was how she expressed it. He had a very quiet little wife who did not count. And there was a well-known doctor who was one of the community of the Scots kirk, and often called on Sabbath mornings to take Miss Jean to Swallow Street in his carriage. Besides these persons, who were her habitual society, there was a floating element of Scotch ladies who were governesses or housekeepers in great families, and who had occasion to know Miss Jean through bringing messages to her from their ladies and being recognized as countrywomen. It was a very strongly Scots society in the middle of Mayfair, very racy of Scotch soil, and full of Scotch ideas though living exclusively in London. It had been a little humiliating to Kirsteen herself to meet them, with the strong conviction she had in her mind that she herself with her good blood must be very much above this little assembly. But she had been obliged to confess that they had all been very agreeable, and old Mrs. Gordon had quoted her fine relations to so much purpose that Kirsteen had been much ashamed of her instinctive resistance and foregone conclusion. All the same she did not think Glendochart would be elated by such an invitation, or that he would consider it a privilege to introduce his wife to the circle at Chapel

Street. His wife! She thought with a momentary thrill that she might have been that important personage, ordering new gowns from Miss Jean instead of sewing under her, driving about in a handsome carriage and doing just what she pleased, with an adoring slave in attendance. And that he should have taken Mary in her place! And that Mary should possess all that had been intended for Kirsteen! She thought she could see the quiet triumph that would be in her sister's eyes, and the way in which she would parade her satisfaction. And wherefore not? Kirsteen said to herself. Since she had paid the price, why should she not have the satisfaction? But it cost Kirsteen an effort to come to this Christian state of mind—and she did not reply to Mary's letter. For indeed she was not at all a perfect young woman, but full of lively and impatient feelings, and irritability and self-opinion—as belonged to her race.

CHAPTER XIV.

LONDON was more than *throng* when Glendochart and his young wife arrived. It was mad with joy over the great battle of Waterloo which had just been fought, and the triumph of the British arms, and the end of the war which nobody had been sure might not be another long war like that of the Peninsula. When the pair from the Highlands reached town, travelling in the coach for Mary thought a postchaise an unnecessary expense, they met, a short distance from London, the coach which carried the news, all decorated with laurels, the conductor performing triumphant tunes upon his horn, the passengers half crazy with shouting, and feeling themselves somehow a part of the victory if not the first cause, flinging newspapers into passing carriages, and meeting every wayfarer with a chorus only half intelligible about the Great and Glorious Victory. The bride was much excited by these announcements. She concluded that now there would be nothing but balls and parties in London, and that Glendochart would receive sheaves of invitations from all quarters; and finally that it was quite essential she should go at once to Miss Jean Brown's, not only to ask after Kirsteen, but to get herself one or two gowns that should be in the height of the fashion and fit to appear at the dinner table of the Duke and Duchess, who she made no doubt would make haste to invite so important a member of the clan. "That will no doubt be the first place we will go to," she said to her husband. "Oh, yes, my dear; if his Grace thinks about it I have no doubt he will mention it to the Duchess, and if they should happen to have a free day——" "Is that all you say, Glendochart, and me a bride?" cried

Mary. But the old bridegroom, who was more or less a man of the world, would not promise more. And he was as much excited by the news as any one, and from the moment when he could seize one of the papers that were flying about, and read for himself the brief dispatch from the field of battle, there was nothing else to be got from him. There was another old soldier in the coach, and the two began to reckon up the regiments that had been engaged and to discuss the names of the officers, and to speculate on the results of this great and decisive victory, and whether Boney would ever hold up his head again. Mary felt almost deserted as she sat back in her corner and found all the caresses and whispers of the earlier journey stopped by this sudden excitement. She did not herself care very much for the victory nor understand it, though she was glad it was a victory. She was half glad also, and half sorry, that none of the boys were with Lord Wellington—sorry that she was deprived of the consequence of having a brother with the army, yet glad that she was thus free of the sad possibility of being plunged into mourning before her honeymoon was over.

But when these thoughts had passed through her mind, Mary turned to her own concerns which were more interesting than any public matters. Flags were flying everywhere as they drove through the streets and a grand tumult of rejoicing going on. The very sound of it was exhilarating, the great placards that were up everywhere with the news, the throngs at every corner, the newsvendors who were shouting at the top of their voices imaginary additions to the dispatches and further details of the victory, the improvised illuminations in many windows, a candle stuck in each pane after the fashion of the time, that to a stranger from the country had a fine effect seen through the smoky haze of the London streets, which even in June and at the beginning of the century was sufficiently apparent to rural perceptions. Mary was not carried away by this fervour of popular sentiment as her old husband was, who was ready to shout for Wellington and the army on the smallest provocation, but she was agreeably stimulated in her own thoughts. She already saw herself at the grand dinners which would be given in celebration of the event in the Duke's great mansion in Portman Square—not placed perhaps by his side, as would in other circumstances have been her right as a bride, but yet not far off, in the midst of the lords and ladies; or perhaps his Grace, who was known to be punctilious, would give her her right whoever was there, were it even a princess of the blood, and she would have the pride and the felicity of looking down upon half the nobility seated below her at the feast. The chief of Glendochart's name could scarcely do less to one of the Douglases entering his clan at such a moment. Mary lay back in her corner, her mind floating away on a private strain of beatific anticipation, while Glendochart hung half out of the window in his excitement, cheering and asking questions. She imagined the princess of the blood, who no doubt would be present, asking of the Duke who the young lady was in her bridal dress who occupied the place of honour, and hearing that she was one of the Douglases, just entered into his Grace's connection by her marriage with Glendochart, the princess then (she almost saw it!) would request to have the bride presented to her, and would ask that the Duchess should bring her one day to Windsor perhaps to be presented to Queen Charlotte, or to Hampton Court or some other of the royal palaces. Mary's heart beat high with this supposition, which seemed more or less a direct consequence of Waterloo, as much so as Boney's downfall, and much more satisfactory than that probable event.

When they arrived in the city where the coaches from the north stopped, and she had to get out, somewhat dazed by all the tumult round her, and the crowd, and the struggle for baggage, and the absence of any coherent guidance through that chaos of shouting men and stamping horses, and coaches coming and going, and everywhere the shouts of the great and glorious victory. Mary was in the act of receiving a pressing invitation from the princess to pass a week with her and meet all the first people in London. She was half annoyed to be disturbed in the midst of these delightful visions, but comforted herself with the thought that it was but a pleasure deferred.

And it may be imagined that with all this in her mind it became more than ever important to Mary to make an early call upon Miss Jean and provide herself as rapidly as possible with a dress that was fit to be worn among such fine company. The riding-habit which she had worn at her marriage, though exceedingly fine and becoming, was not a garment in which she could appear at the dinner-table in Portman Square. There are some rare geniuses who have an intuitive knowledge of what is finest and best without having learned it, and in respect to society and dress and the details of high life Mary was one of these gifted persons. Her habit had been very highly thought of in the country. It was a costume, many rustic persons supposed, in which it would be possible to approach the presence of Queen Charlotte herself. But Mary knew by intuition just how far this was possible. And she knew that for the Duke's table a white gown was indispensable in which to play her part as a bride; therefore, as there was no saying at what moment the invitation might arrive, nor how soon the dinner might take place, she considered it expedient to carry out her intention at once. Happily Glendochart next morning was still a little crazy about the victory, and anxious to go down to the Horse Guards to make inquiries, if she would excuse him, as he said apologetically. Mary did so with the best grace in the world. "And while you are asking about your old friends," she said, "I will just go and see if I can find out anything about my poor sister—" "That is just a most kind thing to do, and exactly what I would have expected from you, my dear," said Glendochart, grateful to his young wife for allowing him so much liberty. And he hastened to secure a glass coach for her in which she could drive to Miss Jean, and "see all the London ferlies," as he said, on the way. It was not a very splendid vehicle to drive up to Miss Jean's door, where the carriages of the nobility appeared every day; but Mrs. Mary felt herself the admired of all beholders as she drove along the streets, well set up in the middle of the seat as if she had been the queen. Her heart beat a little when she reached the house, with mingled alarm as to Kirsteen's reception of her, and pride in her own superior standing, far above any unmarried person, as Mrs. Campbell of Glendochart. The name did not indeed impress the maid who received her, and who asked twice what it was, begging pardon for not catching it the first time, and suggesting " Lady Campbell of—?" "Mistress Campbell," said Mary. She felt even in that moment a little taken down. It was as if the maid was accustomed to nothing less than my lady. She was so agitated that she did not perceive the name of Miss Kirsteen in connection with that of Miss Brown upon the brass plate of the door.

She had, however, quite recovered herself before Kirsteen appeared in the showroom to answer the summons, and advanced rustling in all her new ribbons to meet her sister. "Oh, Kirsteen, is that you? Oh, are you really here? I thought I could not be deceived about Miss Jean harbouring ye and helping ye, but I did not think I would just find ye in a moment like this."

"Yes," said Kirsteen, "I am here, and I have been here ever since I left home."

"Ye have turned quite English, Kirsteen, in the time ye've been away."

"Have I? It's perhaps difficult to avoid

it—if ye have anything of an ear for music." This was perhaps an unkind thing to say, for it was well-known in the family that Mary had no ear for music and could not " turn a tune" to save her life. With a compunction Kirsteen turned to a more natural subject. "And how is my mother?"

"Oh," said Mary, "she is just wonderfully well for her. The marriage was a great divert to her, settling how it was to be and the clothes and everything. She was dressed herself in a new gown that Glendochart presented to her for the occasion, with white ribbons in her cap, and looking just very well. 'It's easy to see where ye get your looks from,' Henry said to me: which I thought was a very pretty compliment to both of us, for if ever a man was pleased with his wife's looks it should be on his wedding-day."

"Very likely," said Kirsteen drily, "but I have no experience. I got your letter, with an account of what you had on."

"Yes, it was considered very becoming,"

said Mary. "And Jeanie was just beautiful in a white frock; I will have her with me at Glendochart when she gets a little older, and bring her out, and maybe take her to Edinburgh for a winter that she may have every advantage. I would like her to make a grand marriage, and there is nothing more likely when she's seen as she ought to be in a house like Glendochart."

"I have yet to learn," said Kirsteen with dilating nostrils and quivering lips (for she too intended Jeanie to make a great match, and to marry well, but under her own auspices not her sister's), "I have yet to learn that a Campbell who is the Duke's clanswoman can give credit to a Douglas that comes of the first family of her own name."

"Maybe you think too," said Mary with all the force of ridicule founded on fact, "that the house of Drumcarro is a good place for letting a young thing see the world."

Kirsteen was silenced by this potent

argument, but it by no means softened the irritation in her mind. She had thought of Jeanie as her own, her creation in many ways, between whom and every evil fate she was determined to stand. To have the child taken out of her hands in this calm way was almost more than she could bear. But she compelled herself to patience with a hasty self-argument: Who was she to stand between Jeanie and any advantage—when nobody could tell whether she would be able to carry out her intentions or not? And at all events at the present moment Jeanie being only fourteen there was not much to be done. Mary's smooth voice going on forbade any very continued strain of thought.

"And, Kirsteen, what is to be done about yourself? We would be real willing to do anything in our power—But oh! it was rash—rash of you to run away—for you see by what's happened that it was all a mistake, and that Glendochart——"

Kirsteen's milk-white brow again grew

as red as fire. To have your old lover console himself with your sister is bad enough; but to have her explain to you that your alarm was a mere mistake of vanity, and that the only person who was ridiculous or blamable in the business was only yourself, ——this is too much for mortal flesh and blood!

"I am much obliged to you," she said with self-restraint which was painful, "but I am very happy where I am. It was no mistake so far as I am concerned. It was just impossible to live on down yonder without occupation, when there are so many things to be done in the world."

"Dear me!" cried Mary astonished with this new view. But at this moment Miss Jean fortunately came in, and was very happy to see the lady of Glendochart and very anxious to show her every attention.

"I consider it a great honour," said Miss Jean, "that you should come to see me the first morning; though well I know it's not for me but for one that is far more worthy. Miss Kirsteen is just the prop of this house, Mistress Campbell. Not a thing can be done without her advice—and though I had little reason to complain, and my basket and my store had aye prospered just wonderful, it's a different thing now Miss Kirsteen is here, for she makes all the fine ladies stand about."

"Dear me," said Mary again, "and how can she do that?" But she was more anxious about her own affairs than the gifts and endowments of her sister. "There is one thing I must say," she added, "before we go further, and that is that I am wishing to get a new gown; for we will likely be asked to our dinner at the Duke's, and though I have all my wedding outfit I would like to be in the newest fashion and do my husband credit with the chief of his name. So perhaps you would show me some white silks, just the very newest. And I would like it made in the last fashion; for Glendochart is very liberal and he will wish me to spare no expense. Being Marg'ret's sister, as well as having been so kind to Kirsteen, it was just natural that I should choose what little custom I have to give into your hands. But I would want it very quickly done, just as quick as the needles can go—for we cannot tell for what day the invitation might come."

Miss Jean with a smile upon her face, the smile with which she received an order, and a bow of acquiescence which made the ribbons tremble in her cap, had taken a step towards the drawers in which her silks were kept; but there was something in Kirsteen's eyes which made her hesitate. She looked towards her young associate with a half-question—though indeed she could not tell what was the foundation of her doubt, in her eyes.

"Miss Jean," said Kirsteen promptly, "you have then forgotten our new rule? You will maybe think I want you to break it in consideration of my sister? But ye need not depart from your regulations out of thought for me. And I am sure I am very sorry," she said turning to Mary, who stood expectant with a smile of genial patronage on her face—" but it's not possible. Miss Jean has made a rule to take no orders from commoners—except them that have been long upon her list. It would just be hopeless if we were to undertake it," Kirsteen said.

"No orders—from commoners?" cried Mary in consternation and wrath.

"Just that; we would have all London at our tails, no to speak of persons from the country like yourself—just pursuing us night and day—if we were to relax our rule. And there are many of the nobility," said Kirsteen turning to Miss Jean with a look of serious consultation, "whom I would wish to be weeded out —for there are titles and titles, and some countesses are just nobodies however much they may think of themselves. You will never get to the first rank," continued Kirsteen, still addressing Miss Jean, "unless ye just settle and never depart from it, who you are to dress, and who not."

"Do you mean, Miss Jean," cried Mrs. Campbell of Glendochart, "that ye will not make me my gown?"

Miss Jean was torn asunder between natural politeness and proper subjection to her superiors, and a still more natural partisanship, not to speak of the glance of fiery laughter in Kirsteen's eyes. "What can I do," she cried, "when you hear with your own ears what Miss Kirsteen has said? I am wae to put you to any inconvenience, but it's just true that we cannot get through the half of our work—and we've plenty with the nobility and old customers to keep us always very *throng*. But I could recommend ye to another person that would willingly serve ye though I cannot take your order myself."

"Oh, I'll find somebody," said Mary in great offence. "It cannot be that in the great town of London you will not get whatever you want when you have plenty of money in your hand."

"No doubt that's very true," said Miss Jean, "and ye may find that ye are not in such a great hurry as ye think, for the Duchess has a number of engagements upon her hands, and will not dine at home for about ten days to my certain knowledge—and probably she will have her table full then if ye have not already received your invitations— for town is just very *throng*, and everything settled for the grand parties, weeks before."

CHAPTER XV.

Miss Jean it must be allowed turned to her young companion with some dismay when Mrs. Campbell of Glendochart had been ceremoniously seen to her hackney coach, and deeply cast down and discomfited, had driven away to the respectable person who had been recommended to her to make her new gown. "Were you meaning yon?" Miss Jean asked with solicitude. "Or what were you meaning?"

"I was meaning what I said," cried Kirsteen holding her head high and with an unusual colour upon her cheeks. "You know yourself that we have more work than can be done if we were to sit at it day and night."

"For the moment," said Miss Jean prudently; "but to refuse work just goes to my heart—it might spoil the business."

"It will do the business good," said Kirsteen. "We will let it be known, not just yet perhaps, what I said, that we will take no commoners' orders—that persons who are nobodies need not come here. You did not take me with you into the business just to go on like other folk."

"No—that's quite true," said Miss Jean, but with a little hesitation still.

"By the time," said Kirsteen, "that you have turned away half-a-dozen from your door, your name will be up over all the town; and whether in the season or out of it, you will have more to do than you can set your face to, and thanks for doing it. Will you trust me or not, Miss Jean? For I allow that I am inexperienced and perhaps I may not be right."

"It would be very strange if ye were always right," said Miss Jean with a smile of affectionate meaning, "for all so young and so sure as ye are. But ye have a great spirit and there's something in me too that just answers till ye. Yes, I'll trust ye, my dear; and ye'll just go insulting all the poor bodies that are not good enough to please ye, till ye make a spoon or spoil a horn for yourself; for it does not matter so very much for me."

"Not the poor bodies," said Kirsteen, "but the folk with money and nothing else, that come in as if they were doing us a favour—women that Marg'ret would not have in her kitchen; and they will come in here and give their orders as if it was a favour to you and me! I would like to learn them a lesson: that though we're mantua-makers, it's not for the like of them —a person with no name to speak of— and giving her orders to one of the Douglases! We will learn them better before we are done."

"Oh pride, pride!" said Miss Jean, " there's something in me that answers till ye, though well I wot I have little to be proud of; but these half and half gentry they are just insufferable to me too."

In all this there was nothing said of Mrs. Mary, to whom none of these descriptions applied, for she was of course one of the Douglases as well as her sister, and Glendochart was as good a gentleman as any of his name. But while Miss Jean Brown, the daughter of a Scotch ploughman, felt something in her that answered to the pride of the well-born Highland girl, there was much in the other that resembled the " half and half gentry," of whom the experienced mantua-maker had seen many specimens. Miss Jean's prognostics however were carried into effect with stern certainty in the disappointment of the country visitors. They did indeed dine in Portman Square, but chiefly because of Lady Chatty's desire to see the personages of the story which she was so fond of telling, and then only on a Sunday evening when the family were alone. Alone, or all but alone, for there was one guest to meet them in the person of Miss

Kirsteen Douglas, who was not a stranger in the house nor awkward, as the bride was in her new gown and much overdressed for the family party. It was impossible for Kirsteen to meet Glendochart, whose wooing had been of so much importance in her life, without a warmer tinge of colour and a slight shade of consciousness. But the good man was so completely unaware of any cause for feeling, that she came to herself with a little start and shock, which was highly salutary and chastised that pride which was Kirsteen's leading quality at this period of her career. Glendochart was so completely married, so pleased with his young wife, and with himself for having secured her, that all former dreams had departed totally from his mind—a discovery which Kirsteen made instantaneously so soon as their eyes met, and which went through and through her with angry amazement, consternation, wonder, mingled after a little while with a keen humorous sense of the absurdity of the situation. He came after dinner and talked to her a little about her circumstances, and how difficult it was to know what to do. "For your father is a very dour man, as Mary says, and having once passed his word that you are never to enter his door, it will be hard, hard to make him change. You know how obdurate he has been about Anne; but we will always be on the watch, and if the time ever comes that a word may be of use——"

"I beg you will take no trouble about it, Glendochart. I knew what I was risking; and but for my mother I have little to regret. And she has not been any the worse," Kirsteen said, almost with bitterness. Nobody seemed to have been the worse for her departure, not even her mother.

"No, I believe she has been none the worse. She is coming to pay us a visit so soon as we get back."

Kirsteen could have laughed, and she could have cried. She could have seized upon this precise, well-got-up elderly gentleman and given him a good shake. To think that she should have been frightened almost out of her wits, and flung all her life to the winds, because of him; and that he was here advising her for her good, as well satisfied with Mary as he ever could have been with herself!

Miss Jean proved however a true prophet in respect to the disappointment of the newly-married couple with their reception in London, and their willingness eventually to accept the hospitality of the mantua-maker, and meet her friends, the minister, the doctor, the silk-mercer, and the old lady of quality, at her comfortable table. Miss Jean gave them a supper at which all these highly respectable persons were present, along with another who gave a character of distinction to the assembly, being no less a person than young Captain Gordon, promoted on the field of battle and sent home with dispatches, the son of the old lady above mentioned, who was not too grand, though all the fine houses in London were open to him, to come with his mother, covering her with glory in the eyes of the humbler friends who had been kind to her poverty. This encounter was the only one which brought Glendochart and his wife within the range of the commotion which was filling all society and occupying all talk. Afterwards, when they returned home, it was the main feature of their record, what Captain Gordon had said, and his account of the battle—"which, you see, we had, so to speak, at first hand; for he got his promotion upon the field, and was sent home with dispatches, which is only done when a young man has distinguished himself; and a near connection of the Huntly family." I am not sure that Mary did not allow it to be understood that she had met this young hero at the Duke's table in Portman Square, but certainly she never disclosed the fact that it was at the mantua-maker's in Chapel Street, Mayfair. Captain Gordon proved to be of much after importance in the family, so that the mode of his first introduction cannot be without interest. The old lady who patronized Miss Jean by sharing her Sunday dinners, and many other satisfactory meals, felt herself, and was acknowledged by all, to have amply repaid her humble friend by bringing this brilliant young hero fresh from Waterloo to that entertainment, thus doing Miss Jean an honour which " the best in the land " coveted. Alick, so far as he was concerned, made himself exceedingly agreeable. He fought the great battle over again, holding his auditors breathless; he gave the doctor details about the hospitals, and told the minister how the army chaplain went among the poor Highlanders from bed to bed. And he accepted an invitation from Glendochart for the shooting with enthusiasm. " But they will want you at Castle Gordon," said the proud mother, desirous to show that her son had more gorgeous possibilities. " Then they must just want me," cried the young soldier. " They were not so keen about me when I was a poor little ensign." Everything was at the feet of the Waterloo hero, who was in a position to snap his fingers at his grand relations and their tardy hospitality. Kirsteen in particular was attracted by his cheerful looks and his high spirit, and his pleasure in his independence and promotion. It was in accord with her own feeling. She said that he put her in mind of her brothers in India—all soldiers, but none of them so fortunate as to have taken part in such a great decisive battle; and thought with a poignant regret how it might have been had Ronald Drummond continued with Lord Wellington's army instead of changing into the Company's service. It might have been he that would have been sent over with the dispatches, and received with all this honour and renown—and then!—Kirsteen's countenance in the shade where she was sitting was suffused with a soft colour, and the tears came into her eyes.

"They get plenty of fighting out there," said the young soldier, who was very willing to console the only pretty girl in the room; "and if it's not so decisive it may be just as important in the long run, for India is a grand possession—the grandest of all. I will probably go there myself, Miss Douglas, for though Waterloo's a fine thing, it will end the war, and what's a poor soldier lad to do?"

"You will just find plenty to do in your own country, Alick," said his mother eagerly.

"Barrack duty, mother! it's not very exciting—after a taste of the other."

"A taste!" said the proud old lady. "He's just been in everything, since the time he put on his first pair of trews. I know those outlandish places, as if they were on Deeside, always following my soldier laddie—Vimiera, and Badajos, and down to Salamanca and Toulouse in France. I could put my finger on them in the map in the dark," she cried with a glow of enthusiasm; then falling into a little murmur of happy sobbing, "God be thanked they're all over," she cried, putting her trembling hand upon her son's arm.

"Amen!" said the minister, "to the final destruction of the usurper and the restoring of law and order in a distracted land!"

"We'll just see how long it lasts," said the doctor, who was a little of a free thinker, and was believed to have had sympathies with the Revolution.

"We'll have French tastes and French fashions in again, and they're very ingenious with their new patterns it must be allowed," said the silk-mercer; "but it will be an ill day for Spitalfields and other places when the French silks are plentiful again."

"There's ill and good in all things. You must just do your best, Miss Jean, to keep British manufactures in the first place," the minister said. "It's astonishing in that way how much the ladies have in their hands."

"Were you at Salamanca—and Toulouse?" said Kirsteen in her corner, where she kept as far as possible from the light of the candles, lest any one should see the emotion in her face.

"Indeed I was, and the last was a field of carnage," said the young soldier. "Perhaps you had a brother there?"

"Not a brother—but a—friend," said Kirsteen, unable to restrain a faint little sigh. The young man looked so sympathetic and was so complete a stranger to her that it was a relief to her full bosom to say a word more. "I could not but think," she added in a very low tone, "that but for that weary India—it might have been him that had come with glory—from Waterloo."

"Instead of me," said the young soldier with a laugh. "No, I know you did not mean that. But also," he added gravely, "both him and me we might have been left on the field where many a fine fellow lies."

"That is true, that is true!" Kirsteen did not say any more; but it flashed across her mind how could she know that he was not lying on some obscure field in India where lives were lost, and little glory or any advantage that she knew of gained?

This gave her, however, a very friendly feeling to young Gordon, between whom and herself the tie of something which was almost like a confidence now existed. For the young man had easily divined what a friend meant in the guarded phraseology of his country-woman.

It was not till long after this that there came to Kirsteen a little note out of that far distance which made amends to her for long waiting and silence. The letter was only from Robbie, whose correspondence with his sisters was of the most rare and fluctuating kind, yet who for once in a way, he scarcely himself knew the reason why, had sent Kirsteen a little enclosure in his letter to his mother, fortunately secured by Marg'ret, who was now everything—nurse, reader, and companion to the invalid. Robbie informed his sister that Jeanie's letter about old Glendochart had "given him a good laugh," and that he thought she was very right to have nothing to say to an old fellow like that. Before the letter arrived there was already a son and heir born in Glendochart house, but Robbie was no further on in the family history than to be aware of the fact that Kirsteen had gone away rather than have the old lover forced upon her. He told her how on the march he had passed the station where Ronald Drummond was, "if you mind him, he is the one that left along with me—but you must mind him," Robbie continued, "for he was always about the house the last summer before I came away."

He was keen for news of home, as we all are when we meet a friend in this place. And I read him a bit of Jeanie's letter which was very well written, the little monkey, for a little thing of her age; how old Glendochart followed you about like a puppy dog, and how you would never see it, though all the rest did. We both laughed till we cried at Jeanie's story. She must be growing a clever creature, and writes a very good hand of writing too. But it was more serious when we came to the part where you ran away in your trouble at finding it out. I hope you have come home by this time and have not quarrelled with my father; for after all it never does any good to have quarrels in a family. However I was saying about Ronald that he was really quite as taken up as I was with Jeanie's letter, and told me I was to give you his respects, and that he would be coming home in a year or two, and would find you out whether you were at Drumcarro or wherever you were, and give you all the news about me, which I consider very kind of him, as I am sure you will do—and he bid me to say that he always kept the little thing he found in the parlour, and carried it wherever he went: though when I asked what it was he would not tell me, but said you would understand: so I suppose it was some joke between you two. And that's about all the news I have to tell you, and I hope you'll think of what I say about not quarrelling with my father. I am in very good health and liking my quarters—and I am,

Your affect. brother,
R. D.

If this had been the most eloquent love-letter that ever was written, and from the hand of her lover himself, it is doubtful whether it would have more touched the heart of Kirsteen than Robbie's schoolboy scrawl, with its complete unconsciousness of every purpose, did. It was the fashion of their time when correspondence was difficult and dear and slow, and when a young man with nothing to offer was too honourable to bind for long years a young woman who in the meantime might change her mind;

although both often held by each other with a supreme and silent faithfulness. The bond, so completely understood between themselves with nothing to disclose it to others, was all the dearer for never having been put into words; although it was often no doubt the cause of unspeakable pangs of suspense, of doubt—possibly of profound and unspeakable disappointment if one or the other forgot. Kirsteen read and re-read Robbie's letter as if it had been a little gospel. She carried it about with her, for her refreshment at odd moments. There came upon her face a softened sweetness, a mildness to the happy eyes, a mellowing beauty to every line. She grew greatly in beauty as her youth matured, the softening influence of this sweet spring of life keeping in check the pride which was so strong in her character, and the perhaps too great independence and self-reliance which her early elevation to authority and influence developed. And everything prospered with Kirsteen. Miss Jean's business became the most flourishing and important in town. Not only commoners, whom she had so haughtily rejected, but persons of the most exalted pretensions had to cast away their pride and sue for the services of Miss Brown and Miss Kirsteen; and as may be supposed, the more they refused, the more eager were the customers at their door. Before Kirsteen was twenty-seven, the fortune which she had determined to make was already well begun, and Miss Jean in a position to retire if she wished with the income of a statesman. This prosperous condition was in its full height in the midst of the season, the workroom so *throng* that relays of seamstresses sat up all night, there being no inspectors to bring the fashionable mantua-makers under control, when the next great incident happened in the life of our Kirsteen.

END OF VOL. II.

www.ingramcontent.com/pod-product-compliance
Lightning Source LLC
Chambersburg PA
CBHW031252250426
43672CB00029BA/2183